W9-BHS-852

RURAL-URBAN CONSOLIDATION

Rural-Urban Consolidation:

THE MERGER OF GOVERNMENTS IN THE BATON ROUGE AREA

William C. Havard, Jr.

and

Floyd L. Corty

Louisiana State University Press

Library of Congress Catalog Card Number: 64-15878
Manufactured in the United States of America by
Cushing-Malloy, Inc., Ann Arbor, Michigan

Published with the assistance of the Agricultural Experiment Station and Bureau of Public Administration at Louisiana State University in cooperation with Farm Production Economics Division, Economics Research Service, United States Department of Agriculture.

Preface

THIS BOOK is a manifestation of the increased involvement of land-grant universities in public affairs. It is unique in that it represents the joint efforts of the Bureau of Public Administration, Department of Government (College of Arts and Sciences), and the Department of Agricultural Economics and Agribusiness (Agricultural Experiment Station, College of Agriculture) of Louisiana State University in cooperation with the Farm Production Economics Division, Economic Research Service of the United States Department of Agriculture. The mandate of the state university is to serve the public in all segments of activity in all areas of the state. This study represents one such service in the area of public affairs particularly in the field of rural-urban relationships.

The authors describe the structure and operations of the parish (county) and city governments of Baton Rouge before and after their consolidation in 1949. The before and after costs are also analyzed, and although costs per capita were found to be higher after consolidation, it is reasonable to assume that without consolidation equivalent services would have been even more costly.

The general evaluation by the authors indicates that, although the system as it now exists is not perfect in all aspects, it has been successful. They conclude: "In terms of the development of new services and expansion of existing services to meet piled-up needs, the record under consolidation is impressive." Furthermore, "the system . . . demonstrates some capacity for the self-correction of weaknesses and possible adaptability to further consolidation."

CHARLES W. UPP
Director, Agricultural Experiment Station

Acknowledgments

GRATEFUL ACKNOWLEDGMENT is extended to the many individuals who helped make this work possible. Particular recognition is given to Mr. Elwood Sartain, the Parish Clerk, who enthusiastically supplied essential information, as well as provided the necessary entree to the many local government agencies involved in this appraisal. Mr. Gordon Kean, Parish Attorney, and Mr. Richard McEwen, Planning Director, read the manuscript and offered useful suggestions. Other personnel in the various public offices were most helpful in making data available. Although subjected to frequent inquiries and interruptions of their normal activities, they were graciously cooperative. The offices most frequently invaded were those of the assessor, sheriff, treasurer, planning and zoning, city-parish clerk, and supervisor of public funds.

The tedious tasks of tabulating and computing financial data and preparing illustrations for this publication were capably performed by student helper Bryce Malone. Valuable research contributions were made by graduate students in the Department of Government: Richard Murray gathered much of the data on public works, and Martin Simmons prepared a preliminary report on planning. We also acknowledge a debt of gratitude to Donald G. Rhodes, a former graduate student, for his thorough background survey of the development of the plan of government. Appreciation is also expressed to Mrs. Elizabeth E. Nelson, Miss Josephine Scurria, and Mrs. Bonnie B. Elliott for their patience in typing early drafts of this work, and to Miss Mildred Cobb for preparing copies of the manuscript for review.

WILLIAM C. HAVARD
FLOYD L. CORTY

Contents

Figures

Tables

RURAL-URBAN CONSOLIDATION

Chapter I

The Problem

SOME OF THE most critical problems of American government in the twentieth century have resulted from the rapid development of metropolitan areas. Difficulties arose in consequence of this growth because metropolitan communities superimposed themselves on older governmental units and on political boundaries which were designed to serve quite different types of communities. The United States has traditionally used three main types of local government units: (1) the county, which serves as an administrative subdivision of the state and performs certain limited functions of local government which have been related, for the most part, to rural areas; (2) municipalities, which are incorporated areas whose governments operate under charters granted by the states, with powers especially designed to cope with urban needs and services; and (3) town units (mostly in New England), which may or may not be incorporated, but usually include a core village or small city, and the immediately surrounding rural area. In recent years both the older and newer urban areas in the United States have grown with such rapidity that the built-up (urbanized) areas have tended to spill over static city boundaries and beyond the boundaries of the counties in which the central cities are located. In a number of cases urban growth has even crossed state lines. This phenomenon came forcibly to the attention of students of government at least as early as the 1920's, and in the decades since 1940 the situation has reached the point at which metropolitan growth may be said to constitute a continuing crisis in American local government.

For the most part the problem has centered on larger urbanized developments designated by the United States Bureau of the Census as "standard metropolitan areas," but the problem besets some smaller urban communities as well. Although the definition of the standard metropolitan area has varied slightly from census to census (prior to the 1950 census, in fact, such areas were known as "metropolitan districts"), the concept of the metropolitan area is based on counties which contain a central city of at least 50,000 population, together with groups of contiguous counties (or "towns" in New England) which form areas of economic and social interdependence with the core cities. Some indication of the growth of such areas is given by the fact that there were 96 metropolitan districts in the United States in 1930; by 1940 this number had risen to 140, and by 1950 the standard metropolitan areas numbered 168. When the 1960 census was taken the figure had increased to 212. In 1950 for the first time the census demonstrated that more than half of the people of the United States lived in standard metropolitan areas; by 1960 the number of metropolitan area residents had risen to 63 per cent of the national population. The extent to which this growth has tended to expand far beyond the existing boundaries of government units is demonstrated by the fact that today approximately one-half of all the population of the 212 metropolitan areas live outside the corporate boundaries of the central cities which form the core of this type of urbanization. In every census since 1920 population growth outside the corporate limits of the central cities has tended greatly to exceed the growth of population in the central cities themselves. In several sections, such as the northeastern part of the United States, continuous urbanization has expanded so broadly that some of the conglomerations of municipalities have taken on the character of metropolitan regions covering a multiplicity of contiguous counties and spilling over the boundaries of two or more states.

Most observers regard the problems of the urban sprawl outward from the center of a metropolitan area as essentially a single problem with many interrelated (and diversified) parts. That is to say, those who are most familiar with the problems recognize that such invariable accompaniments of urbanization as vast increases in traffic and transportation needs, noise, air pollution, the deterioration of physical structures and coherent community life, and the great increase in the need for urban services of all types require consideration from the standpoint of the overall area, rather than from the point of view of a multiplicity of separate and narrowly confined units of local government of various types. The insights of students of urban development into the need for cohesive organization and action, however, have had little effect on the actual development of local government forms and processes that would produce the potentiality for treating the metropolitan area as a unity. Characteristically, the boundaries and jurisdictions of traditional units of local government have remained rigid, and piecemeal solutions to area-wide problems have been sought through the creation of special districts, the separate incorporation of areas adjacent to existing cities, and similar limited responses to the emerging situation. The result has been a plethora of local government units overlapping and overlying one another and frequently producing conflict, duplication of services, and jealousy of their special prerogatives on the part of each narrow jurisdictional element in the complex. The New York metropolitan region alone contains more than 1,400 separate governmental units, and over 15,000 separate governmental units operate within the defined boundaries of metropolitan areas throughout the United States. These include almost 300 counties, more than 3,500 municipalities, approximately 2,500 townships, and nearly 10,000 school or other special districts.

More than 100 major metropolitan surveys have been taken since 1920 to try to find solutions to the problems which are reflected in this vast proliferation of governmental units and functions. In addition, literally thousands of piecemeal studies have been made of particular problems or special areas within these metropolitan communities. A wide variety of proposals has been offered for coping with this confusion of uncontrolled expansion, but for the most part the recommendations have met with small success in application.

Perhaps the most frequently suggested solution to the problem of runaway urbanization has been annexation by the central city of the surrounding and rapidly growing suburban areas. Although annexation undoubtedly has much to recommend it in terms of providing more effective municipal services at lower costs, in terms of improving property values both inside and outside the city and of unifying the entire area into a community under a single government, several obstacles have stood in the way of the full use of this device for enlarging the city boundaries to take in the entire metropolitan complex. Opposition to a proposed annexation is frequently aroused from outside the city on the ground that taxes will be increased and services will be slow to expand in the newly annexed subdivisions; on the contrary, some cities find themselves reluctant to take in outlying sections of a less desirable type on the grounds that the tax remuneration will not be sufficient to provide for the additional services that have to be extended to the areas taken into the city. The movement to suburban areas is often a deliberate flight from taxes and from the land use regulation and other controls that are essential to orderly municipal development, and suburban residents tend to be suspicious about the political aims and ambitions of municipal governments. More often than not annexation has to take place under statutes requiring a favorable vote on the proposal on the part of both those inside and those outside the city, the result being that annexation proceedings are difficult to initiate and are likely to be narrowly constricted in terms of the territory sought for inclusion in the city. Finally, other incorporated municipalities are frequently to be found within the boundaries of the area proposed for annexation, and it is ordinarily impossible for one incorporated municipality to annex a territory that is already separately incorporated. Some states have liberalized their annexation laws, and large annexations have subsequently been achieved in growing metropolitan areas. However, in most states the possibility of solving the problems of metropolitan growth by annexation simply cannot be or has not been realized.

Several solutions to the metropolitan area problem that are more comprehensive than annexation have been proposed and in some instances, at least, have been acted upon. One of the more interesting recommendations has been to create federated local government systems in heavily urbanized areas that contain a large number of independent units of government. Examples of completely or partially federated metropolitan areas include Toronto, Canada, which developed such a form of government in 1953, and the Miama—Dade County, Florida, federation which went into effect in 1957. Under a federated system, certain local government functions are assigned to a comprehensive central government covering the entire metropolitan complex, while other functions — presumably those less urgently requiring unification — are left to the control of individual municipalities or other units of government within the local complex. The system has the advantage of preserving some of the identities of the local units while consolidating functions that have an obvious area-wide implication. The difficulty of applying the federated principle to metropolitan areas which spill across state lines or to governmental jurisdictions in which the county powers are extremly limited and cannot be enlarged without heroic political effort tend to limit the use of the "federated metropolis" idea in many places.

In some metropolitan areas an attempt has been made to separate the urbanized areas from the surrounding rural countryside by the development of a policy of city-county separation, with the municipal government exercising all the powers traditionally assigned both to city and county governments. Although unification undoubtedly results from this plan, the absence in practically all the areas in which it has been attempted (except perhaps in Virginia) of any means for the separate city to expand its boundaries in order to keep pace with metropolitan growth places the separated municipality in much the same status as other cities which cannot enlarge their boundaries without great difficulties. A related attempt to solve the metropolitan problem has been to vest counties with some powers that normally are assigned to municipalities, thus services of a municipal type may be extended to unincorporated urbanized areas within the county. The biggest disadvantage in this form of consolidated government is the tendency of county governments to remain organizationally adapted to the performance only of rural government services and to be unable to adjust to the type of problems that have to be confronted in urban or suburban areas.

Among the larger metropolitan communities, one of the most frequent efforts to solve major service problems has been to create special metropolitan districts covering large — in some cases intercounty — areas with a view to bringing essential services to the entire metropolitan area. Ordinarily such districts are concerned with a single function, e.g., with sewerage, water, parks, or transportation. The results frequently are the lack of integration of these individual services with other services in the metropolitan area, the proliferation of administrative units and separate taxing authorities,

and a general misunderstanding of functional responsibilities in local government on the part of local residents. In some instances, however, the use of large single-function districts has provided considerable flexibility in crossing established local governmental lines and in integrating some major functions of government. The New York Port Authority, for example, which is based on an interstate compact, performs a wide variety of functions relating to transportation for the whole New York City–Northern New Jersey metropolitan complex.

Of all the attempted solutions to the metropolitan area problem, the one which is of most immediate concern for the purposes of this study is city-county consolidation. Under this plan the ordinarily separate governments of the county and the city or cities which lie within the county are brought into a single metropolitan governmental system. This merger of governments does not necessarily imply that some separate governments may not continue to exist in a manner similar to the solution envisaged in the federated metropolitan district. However, city-county consolidation usually implies a much greater degree of unification of both governmental organization and the administration of major local functions than does federation. City-county consolidation has greatest applicability to those areas in which virtually all of the urbanized development lies within the boundaries of a single county; it hardly suits the needs of metropolitan areas which spill over county lines, especially where, as is usually the case, county boundaries cannot be altered with any facility. City-county consolidation has the obvious advantage of unifying all types of previously separate governmental entities into one single government with responsibility for the whole area. It also offers the advantage of providing the necessary room for orderly urban expansion by including both urbanized and rural areas within the confines of a single governmental jurisdiction. A great many attempts have been made to provide for the consolidation of city and county governments in many parts of the United States. In recent years two successful examples of the application of this type of solution to metropolitan government may be cited – the case of the City of Baton Rouge and East Baton Rouge Parish (county) in Louisiana, and the City of Nashville and Davidson County in Tennessee.

Although the various attempts to deal with the metropolitan area problem may be grouped under the general categories just cited, in point of fact every attempt to solve a metropolitan problem has to take account of unique features in the particular community; and each successful effort to provide some overall metropolitan government has resulted in a variation in practical experience from place to place, even among communities in which the legal plans of government have been quite similar. Despite the numerous studies that have been carried out with a view to creating more viable governmental patterns in metropolitan areas, only a few proposals for overall change have finally been put into effect. And even in those instances in which major changes in governmental organization have occurred, practically no studies have been made of the overall effectiveness of the governmental plans as they have developed in practice. In order to provide more information of this type, this monograph appraises the operation of the city-parish government in one of the metropolitan communities in which substantial change has been carried out — the metropolitan area of Baton Rouge and East Baton Rouge Parish. The proposed solution to the Baton Rouge metropolitan area problem was a consolidation of the city and parish governments; as it turned out, this was a partial-functional consolidation rather than a complete unification of the two governmental systems.

The original impetus for this review of the operations of local government under the Baton Rouge city-parish consolidation came from the Farm Economics Production Division of the United States Department of Agriculture, which has had a long-standing interest in the effect of metropolitan government on rural areas and on the problems created by the expansion of suburban and other types of development into formerly rural areas. Although the study which follows concentrates heavily on the way in which services under the consolidated government have been developed and extended to the rural areas of the parish, it is obvious that a full appreciation of the effects of the consolidation on the rural area of East Baton Rouge Parish cannot be achieved without going into the overall pattern and operations of the metropolitan government. Accordingly, we have first attempted to outline the governmental situation that existed in East Baton Rouge Parish and in the City of Baton Rouge prior to the consolidation. In this background survey we have tried to indicate some of the planning and persuasive efforts that were necessary to overcome the obstacles toward moving in the direction of a unified metropolitan government. Following this, we have examined the results of the consolidation in the light of more than a decade of experience in its operation. The evaluation of the way in which consolidated government has worked in practice has been attempted by means of a survey of the organization of the city-parish government and of the administrative programs of the most important consolidated departments in the city-parish government. In addition we have made a comparison of the major financial aspects of the new plan of government with the fiscal situation which prevailed under the old separate city and parish governments. Finally, we have assayed some general conclusions about the strengths and weaknesses of the consolidation and offered some broad suggestions about the possible applicability of this particular experience with consolidation to other metropolitan areas.

Although the central focus of our inquiry has been the effects of the consolidation on the rural sectors of the metropolitan parish of East Baton Rouge, we hope that the end result has been a fairly comprehensive survey of the entire metropolitan system in operation. And here we must enter a caveat: we have been concerned solely with the institutional factors and with the services rendered by the new consolidated government as compared to the old separated ones. We make no claims to have made a definitive study of the political attitudes which led to the adoption of the consolidated government or of the attitudes of the metropolitan area residents toward the system which prevails today. As important as this type of survey research might have been in terms of the enhancement of knowledge of local politics, and as much as it may be hoped that such a project will be carried out in the future, our mandate and our aims were much more limited.

Chapter II

City-Parish Consolidation

Introduction

IN 1949 THE City of Baton Rouge and the Parish (county) of East Baton Rouge, in which the city is located, were substantially reorganized in an attempt to cope with the problems of metropolitan growth and development in the area.[1] The reorganization took the form of a limited or partial merger of the parish and city governments; in particular, several of the important functions of local government were consolidated into single departments operating under a governing body that was, for area-wide purposes, unified. An observer has referred to this reorganization as a "compound-functional consolidation."[2] Although the resulting city-parish government is unique in structure and operation, it can still claim to have been the first effective city-county merger in the United States since that of the City of Denver and Arapahoe County in Colorado in 1902.

The reasons behind the consolidation were typical: rapid industrialization and population growth had produced vast sociological changes in the Baton Rouge metropolitan area; these changes called for enlarged governmental services and the existing local government areas and organizations provided no satisfactory basis either for meeting these service needs or for the planning of orderly community development for the future. The governmental inadequacies were not only productive of immediate frustrations in terms of the necessities of urban life, but they were serious enough to cause residents to be apprehensive both about the preservation of the economic gains that the area had already achieved and the curtailment of its potential for future industrial growth. Interest, then, in the Baton Rouge experience is related less to the problems confronting the area (since similar ones face virtually every metropolitan community) than to the fact that this is one of the few communities in which comprehensive governmental change has been effected as part of the effort to resolve the problems of urban sprawl. Despite this achievement, structural and functional changes in government are predicated on, and limited by, experience with existing organizations and practices. Hence, it is useful to have some understanding of the governmental conditions which preceded the change.

Local Government Before 1949

Baton Rouge and Its Environs. The City of Baton Rouge, encompassed by East Baton Rouge Parish, is situated on the east bank of the Mississippi River in that portion of southeast Louisiana known as the Florida Parishes because, until 1810, the territory was part of Spanish West Florida. The city is 150 air miles and 240 river miles from the mouth of the river in the Gulf of Mexico. The climate and topography of the area are favorable to the industrial growth that the parish has experienced during the past two decades. The city, which is about 80 air miles north of New Orleans, is located at the last point on the Mississippi River that is accessible to ocean-going vessels. It also has the benefit of natural protection from floods by virtue of its situation on the first series of river bluffs above the mouth of the Mississippi. Furthermore, the river follows a straight course for approximately eight miles as it passes the city in the stretch known as the "Baton Rouge Reach." At this point the river is approximately a half-mile wide, with a deep channel (35 feet) which offers excellent opportunities for the development of port facilities. The area also enjoys the advantages of the subtropical climate of the Gulf States, an abundant water supply, easy access to a variety of natural resources (especially oil, gas, and sulfur) and a strategic navigational site for both river and ocean traffic.

The Parish of East Baton Rouge was created in 1811, although its boundaries were not completely defined until 1832. It now covers an area of 462 square miles. The City of Baton Rouge was first incorporated in 1817, although town or village settlements existed on the site at least as early as 1719. The legislature met in Baton Rouge as early as 1829, but the city was not established as the capital of the state until the Louisiana Constitutional Convention of 1845. After the Civil War, the state university was moved to Baton Rouge, where it later absorbed the nearby agricultural and mechanical college. Baton Rouge continued to be a small town on the Mississippi River until well into the twentieth century, with its chief claim to prominence resting on the fact that it was the seat of the state government and the locus of the state university. It experienced a steady and substantial growth, but its boundaries had not been enlarged to any appreciable extent. At the time of the city-parish consolidation, the city embraced an area of only 4.6 square miles.

Parish and City Governments. Prior to the 1949 consolidation, the area's local government functions were carried out by the parish government, by the city government of Baton Rouge, by the governments of small incorporated towns in the parish – Baker and Zachary – and by a variety of special (or ad hoc) districts, most of which were organized and operated through the governing authority of the parish. Like most of the other southern states, Louisiana has relied heavily on county or, as it is uniquely known in this state, "parish" government. The parish is a geographical and administrative subdivision of the state, and it really serves a dual governmental function. On the one hand, it is an administrative district of the state within which a variety of state laws may be enforced in a conveniently decentralized manner; on the other hand, it is a quasi corporate unit of government which is empowered to carry out certain local functions within the framework of general delegations of power by the state.[3] The parish was designed primarily for rural governmental purposes; to the extent that it performs services ordinarily considered to be municipal, it does so in response to manifest need and strong demand and not because it was conceived as an instrument for comprehensive local government.

Parish government is diffused among a variety of semiautonomous boards, commissions, and offices. The main governing agency of most Louisiana parishes is the police jury, which is the Louisiana counterpart of the county commission or similar governing agencies in other parts of the county.[4] Police jurors are popularly elected for four-year terms. The state constitution permits the parishes to be divided into not less than five nor more than twelve wards, and police jurors are elected from each of these wards in accordance with a population formula. Prior to 1949, East Baton Rouge Parish contained ten wards: Wards One and Two comprised the City of Baton Rouge, see Figure I. The police jury was composed of seven-

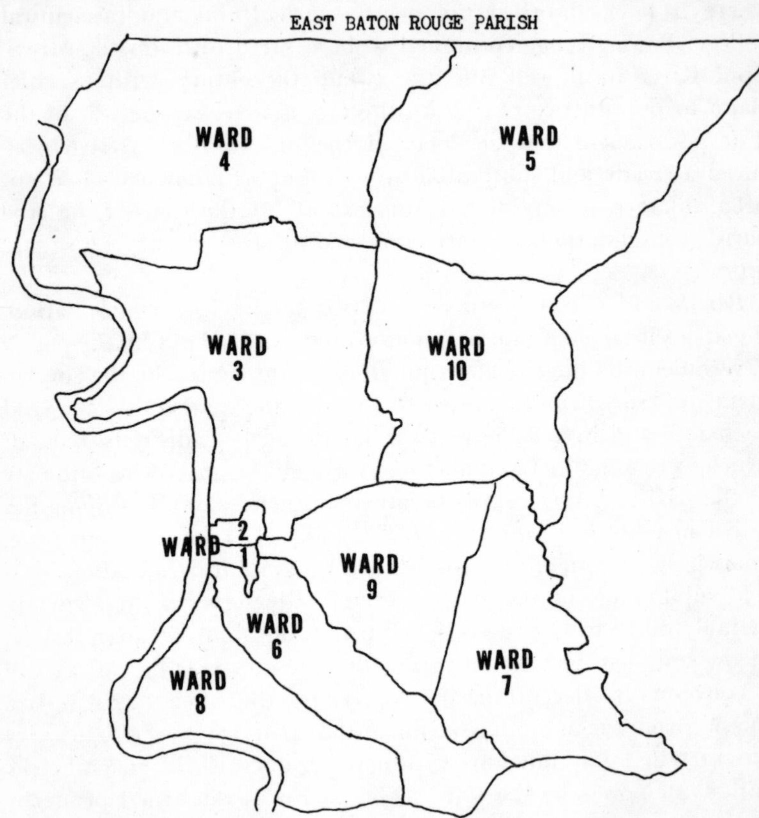

FIGURE I Ward Divisions in East Baton Rouge Parish Prior to Consolidation

teen members elected on a ward basis, each ward having at least one juror and being assigned additional ones for each 10,000 inhabitants, or part thereof over 7,500. In keeping with general practice, the East Baton Rouge Parish police jury selected one of its own members as president and appointed a secretary-treasurer from outside its membership. Members were paid a fixed per diem for each meeting (not to exceed an annual average of one per week), plus travel expenses.

The police jury was responsible for preparing and approving the parish budget, although the autonomous quality of several of the other governing authorities left the police jury little fiscal discretion except in relation to those functions directly under its control.[5] The governmental activities of the police jury related mainly to public works. Of most importance in this respect was the maintenance of the parish road system (including a substantial number of bridges), and drainage. In keeping with usual practice, parish road maintenance and drainage works were carried out almost exclusively on a ward basis, with the police jurors from the respective wards maintaining substantial administrative control over the funds, equipment, and crews that were allocated to these functions. A portion of the state gasoline tax was dedicated to parish road uses, but most of the support for public works came from the authorized parish ad valorem tax of four mills, which was reduced to half this amount within municipalities responsible for their own street maintenance. In addition to its public works function, the police jury had extensive powers to enact regulatory ordinances in functional areas such as livestock control, places of public entertainment, peddling, trespassing, ferries, and toll bridges.

As these duties and responsibilities indicate, the police jury was conceived primarily to meet the limited governmental needs of a rural area. However, the growth of the urban fringe in East Baton Rouge Parish and the absence of other governmental arrangements forced the police jury to provide some municipal services to the suburban communities outside the City of Baton Rouge. For the most part, these services were developed through special or ad hoc districts, although some services, such as garbage collection, were directly provided for out of parish funds for heavily built-up areas, particularly in that portion of the old Ward Three known as North Baton Rouge. Under the constitution and laws of Louisiana, special (single purpose ad hoc) districts can be organized by the police juries for a wide variety of purposes. For the most part, the police jurors from the ward or wards in which these districts are organized serve as their governing authority; they are ordinarily created in response to requests of residents and they are limited by the state constitution and laws in relation to maximum millages, conditions and extent of bonded indebtedness, and permissible functions. Taxes may be levied and debts incurred by these districts only upon approval by a referendum of the qualified voters in the district who are property taxpayers. The accompanying ward map (Figure II)

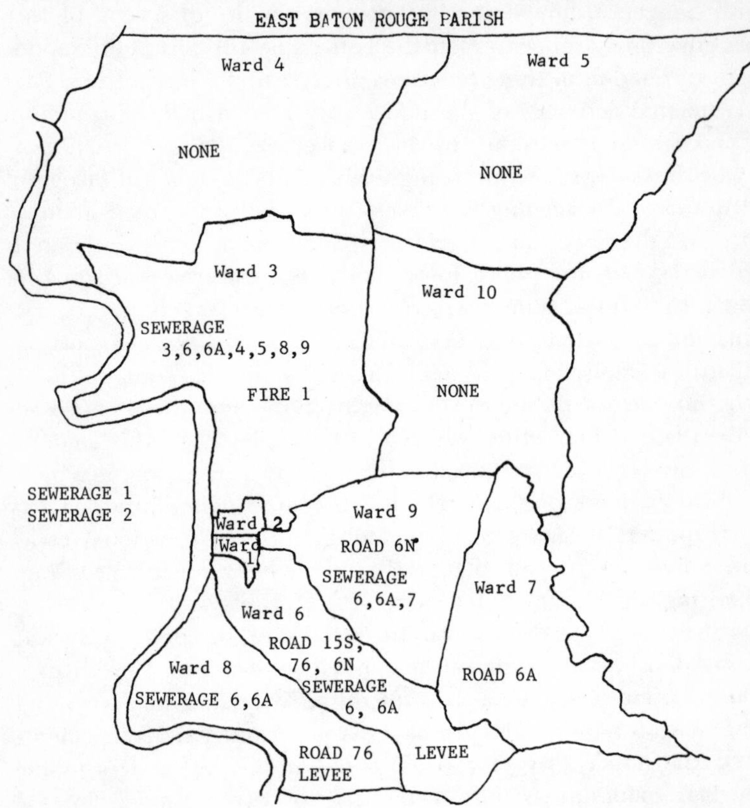

FIGURE II Special Districts in East Baton Rouge before Consolidation

indicates the general location of the special districts in East Baton Rouge Parish as of 1947.[6] The millages applied against the property value base in these various districts ranged from 0.80 mills (sewerage district 4) to 5.50 mills (road district 6N).

In addition to the police jury, Louisiana parishes have several constitutionally established elective officers who perform a variety of administrative functions. These include the sheriff, clerk of the district court, the assessor, and the coroner. All of these officials are elected for a four-year term at the state general election. The sheriff is chief law-enforcement officer as well as ex officio tax collector for state, parish, and municipal taxes (if a city desires it). It is his duty to enforce the state laws and parish ordinances, maintain peace and order, keep the jail, and act as an officer of the district court in preserving order and executing the court's writs. The clerk of court is recorder of court proceedings and custodian of the records of the court and of other important parish records such as marriages and conveyances. The assessor appraises and fixes the value of most property within the parish which is subject to ad valorem taxes levied by the state, parish, municipalities, and special districts. The coroner (who must be a qualified physician if there is one in the parish who is willing to serve) has the duty of investigating sudden or violent deaths of unknown cause; he may hold inquests and autopsies, and he performs the law-enforcement functions of the sheriff when a vacancy occurs in the latter's office or in cases in which the sheriff is an interested party.

The salaries of these officials are set by state law, but in the case of the sheriff and clerk, a substantial portion of the office budget derives from fees collected or withheld during the course of their activities. Thus, although the police jury may be required by state law to supplement (or supply outright) the funds for supporting these offices, the incumbents are not only outside the control of the police jury as independent elective officials, but have a substantial degree of fiscal autonomy as well. By tradition, these offices are so thoroughly ensconced in the governmental system that they continue to exist as popularly elective positions even in those parishes (Orleans, East Baton Rouge, and Jefferson) which have abolished the police jury in favor of parish-wide consolidation of government. These offices function somewhat differently in New Orleans, however.

The administration of public education, welfare, and health programs is centralized to a considerable degree at the state level in Louisiana, and the latter two are of only incidental concern to the problems treated here. It should be noted, however, that the parish administrative units (parish school board, parish welfare board, and city-parish health unit) which have local responsibility for these functions also operate with no supervision, or at most with nominal supervision, by the parish and city councils. For purposes of administering the school districts, the state has provided that each parish shall constitute what amounts to a consolidated local school district; in addition, three municipalities in the state maintain city school districts that are separate from the parish school system in which each is located. In each parish, school board members are, with certain exceptions, equal in number to the membership of the parish governing authority, and they are ordinarily elected from the same wards as are the members of the police jury or other parish governing bodies. However, they are elected at the Congressional, rather than the state, elections,[7] and serve for six-year overlapping terms. The board prepares the parish school budget and submits it for approval of the state budget committee (a special agency for educational purposes which is composed of three major state-elected officials in an ex officio capacity). Although state educational grants for the parishes are high, the parish school boards also levy ad valorem millages within the limits set by the law and include these local levies in their proposed budgets. Once the parish budget is approved at the state level, the board informs the parish governing authority of the millage level of the school tax and this figure is incorporated into the assessor's rolls and then into the sheriff's tax records as part of the total ad valorem taxes to be paid by the property owners. Parish school boards also select teachers for the parish schools, determine the number and location of schools in the parish, and supervise and control the parish public school system within the policy framework of the state. A parish school superintendent is appointed by each school board for a four-year term; the superintendent acts as the chief administrator under the board and serves as its secretary.

With some variations, including somewhat more fiscal and administrative responsibilities to the parish governing authority in the case of the health unit[8] and virtually none in the case of welfare, the parish agencies which administer health and welfare functions are similarly independent of substantial control by the police jury or other parish governing authority. Local administrative discretion in these three areas, then, is limited less by local governing bodies of a general nature than by state government, state law, and the corresponding state administrative department. The state courts also have a relation to the parishes that is of some importance. Some of the district courts cover a multiparish area, but each of a number of the larger parishes comprises a separate district. The Nineteenth Judicial District of the State of Louisiana, for example, is coterminous with East Baton Rouge Parish. Under any circumstances, however, each parish serves as a division for the enforcement of law and preservation of court records, and the judges in a multiparish district hold court in each of the parishes. In addition, the empanelment of juries and some other elements of the court system follow parish boundaries in their organization and functions. Parishes are allowed to organize justice of the peace courts outside the areas of incorporated municipalities for minor civil cases and for criminal cases where the judge is a committing magistrate only. Justices of the peace and the constables of the justice of the peace courts are popularly elected for four-year terms on a ward basis.[9]

Although several additional officials or agencies play some role in parish government, only one other pre-1949 parish-wide administrative organization is sufficiently pertinent to this discussion to be mentioned here, and that is an administrative agency originally called the Baton Rouge Parish and Municipal Recreation Commission. It was organized in 1941, and therefore was the first fully consolidated city-parish agency. The commission was until 1946 little more than an ad hoc body for whose support the city commission of Baton Rouge and the parish police jury made small appropriations if surplus revenues could be found. In 1946, a successor agency, the recreation and park commission of the city and parish, was given constitutional status through an amendment authorizing the legislature to create the agency as a public corporation and subdivision of the state.[10] Upon approval of the property taxpayers of the parish, the commission could incur debt and levy a tax not to exceed one mill on the dollar for the support of its functions. The legislature passed the enabling act establishing the agency in the same session at which the amendment was proposed.[11] Under terms of the act, the police jury and the city commission each appointed three members to the recreation and park commission for overlapping three-year terms; in addition, the parish superintendent of education, the president of the police jury, and the city commissioner of streets and parks served as ex officio members of the agency. The commission was authorized to appoint a superintendent of recreation and parks as the chief administrator of the agency. Corporate powers necessary to enable it to administer the recreation and parks function throughout the parish were vested in the agency; provisions for its financial support were established by an authorization for the agency to levy a property tax and incur debt (within the limits established by the constitutional amendment) provided the tax and debt proposals were approved in a property taxpayers' election.[12] The tax powers of the agency were subsequently approved by the parish electors in a property tax election. In this manner yet another single-purpose agency was established with virtually autonomous governmental powers and an independent financial base.

Prior to 1949, the government of East Baton Rouge Parish, like that in most of the parishes in Louisiana, was spread among a wide variety of administrative agencies. Most of these agencies were narrowly restricted in function; many of them, in fact, were confined to single purposes. Even when an agency had some general governmental responsibilities (as in the case of the police jury), it tended in practice further to disperse its activities by breaking the governing body down into a multiple administrative complex, each unit of which operated in a narrow geographical framework without any attempt to plan, direct, or coordinate administration in relation to the parish as a whole. In contrast, however, with some other areas of the United States, Louisiana has in varying degrees centralized certain functions at the state level, particularly with regard to major policy-making and financing. This has permitted local administrative agencies to operate within the framework of an acceptable policy and over an area that is sufficiently rationalized to produce some degree of efficiency and commonalty of service standards. In education, for example, the state has avoided the problems of the single school district. Even before 1949, East Baton Rouge Parish formed a unified school district within a geographic area that was suitable in terms of population, tax base, and community cohesiveness for effective administration. Despite this advantage, the administration of the public schools lacked much in the way of needed coordination with other public bodies engaged in community development. To cite but one example, the problem of school location is closely related to projected population growth and residential location, overall problems of planning and zoning, transportation and access routes, and recreation. Unless there is a governing body (or governing bodies) capable of assuming responsibility and coordinating these activities for the entire school district, the local school authorities are forced to try to perform their own planning activities in a vacuum, and the number of centers of administrative decision-making through which coordination must be sought tends to be so great as to be unworkable.

From 1914 until 1949, the City of Baton Rouge operated under a commission form of municipal government, after having previously been organized under the mayor-council form. The commission-council consisted of three members elected at large from the incorporated area for four-year terms. Each candidate declared the specific commission post that he sought in the municipal election: the mayor served as commissioner of public health and safety; another commissioner was vice-president of the council with responsibility for finance and utilities; and the third was commissioner of public parks and streets, Figure III. The commissioner of finance also served as city treasurer and tax collector. The council appointed a city attorney, police chief, fire chief, accountant, auditor, civil engineer, and city physician. The city court was presided over by a city judge who was popularly elected. The city provided the usual municipal services of police and fire protection, street maintenance and lighting, garbage collection and, through two municipal districts, sewerage disposal. In addition, of course, the city exercised further police powers in the area of protection of the public health, safety, welfare, and morals of its citizens through a variety of licensing and inspection regulations. Water, electricity, and gas were furnished through private utility companies. There will be occasion later to appraise the extent to which some of these services were effective, but for the moment it is worth noting that the city had no planning agency; largely as a consequence of this hiatus, comprehensive zoning was altogether lacking.

In 1909, the Standard Oil Company of Louisiana located a major refinery at Baton Rouge; in 1920 this plant greatly expanded and diversified its operations as the first stage in what was to be a tremendous development of products from crude oil and residues from its refinement. This expansion heralded Baton Rouge's emergence as a major industrial center. In the late 1930's the Ethyl and Dupont corporations built plants, and these were followed by other industries, primarily, although not altogether, in the petrochemical field. During the defense build-up, preceding and during World War II, some $125 million in capital investments in new plants were made in Baton Rouge. The city draws on a labor market which includes eight other adjacent parishes, with a total population now rising toward half a million people. Before 1920, the

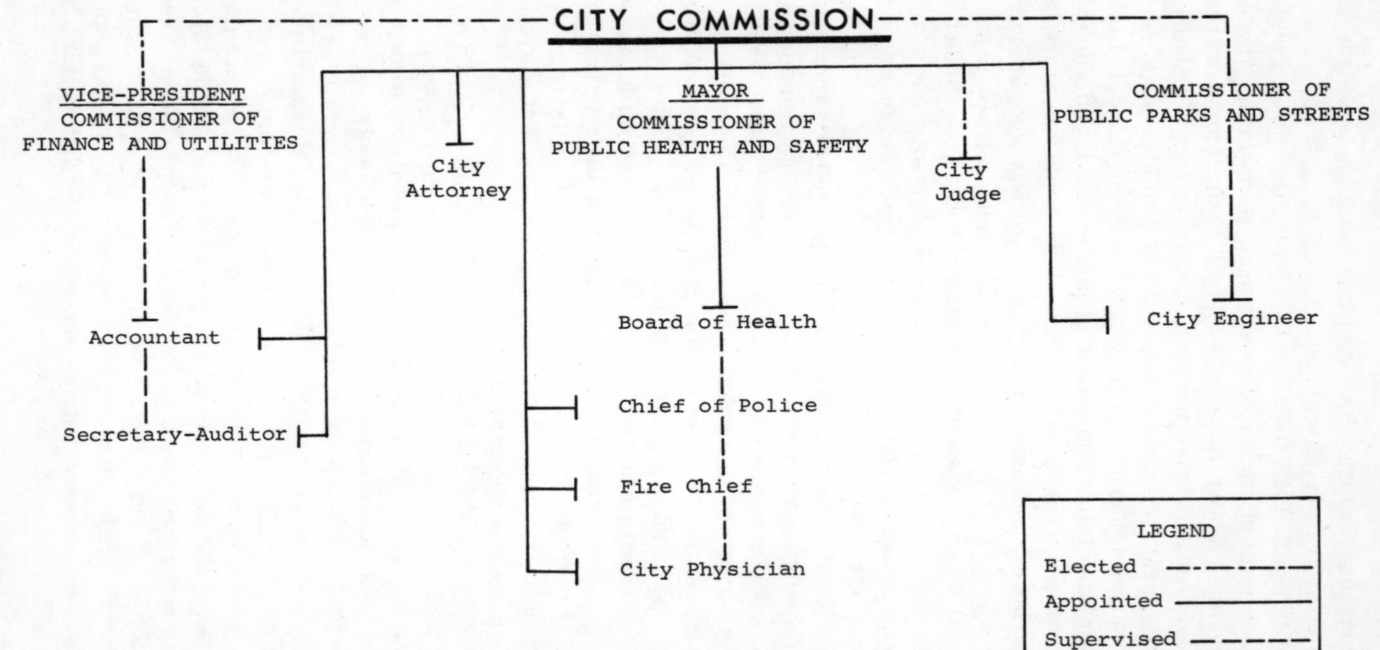

FIGURE III Organization of Baton Rouge Commission Prior to Consolidation

urban growth had been largely confined within the narrow boundaries of the city, with the remainder of the parish population well scattered throughout what was in fact a rural area. After 1920, however, the spill-over assumed major proportions but little was done about the situation. The new urban population growth was concentrated in three areas: the first area was of greatest density and consisted of the residents of subdivisions surrounding the industrial complex adjacent to the northern boundaries of the old city limits; the second was in the near southern section of the parish around the university (which had been moved to a new outlying plantation site in the 1920's); and a third (and more scattered build-up) began to occur east of the old city boundaries in and after the late 1930's. The growth that occurred presented some favorable and some unfavorable attributes insofar as the future of the metropolitan area was concerned. In the first place, the metropolitan area of Baton Rouge was entirely within the boundaries of East Baton Rouge Parish; in this sense it was a unified development rather than a multicounty or even multiurban metropolitan community. The industrial areas were grouped along the Mississippi River to the north of the city and did not intrude on the old residential areas.

In addition to their concentration of location, the types of industries that came in were generally "clean" and highly capitalized in proportion to numbers of persons employed, and they had relatively high wage standards. On the other hand, the lack of effective controls on residential expansion meant that land use patterns created major problems by scattering the population over areas far too broad for effective and economical provision of urban services. Furthermore, none of the governmental organizations in the metropolitan area could effectively undertake to plan for and provide these services on a systematic basis. The parish government which covered the areas where the growth was occurring was oriented to rural conditions and the city government was confined to a fractional portion of the urbanized complex. The conditions which were to give rise to pressures for consolidation were well under way by the time World War II came, and the war situation exacerbated these conditions while frustrating any possibility of a change during its continuation.

The Move Toward Consolidation

The first steps toward doing something about the problems of a metropolitan area without metropolitan government were taken by private groups rather than the city or parish governments in Baton Rouge. This was perhaps indicative of the lack of vitality in the prevailing governmental system. In 1944, the Baton Rouge Chamber of Commerce requested that its committee on economic development undertake a study of the feasibility of replacing the city-commission government and the parish police jury with a unified form of local government. Subsequently, the chamber proposed and undertook the formation of a committee to take the steps necessary to develop a city-parish plan of government which would embrace the entire parish. Pursuant to this end a city-parish "planning commission" of five members (later expanded to eight) was organized, with its representative membership drawn from the chamber of commerce, the City of Baton Rouge (the mayor served), the police jury, the parish school board, and the state department of public works. The committee soon reached the conclusion that a comprehensive city plan was so basic a necessity that it took precedence over any other possible actions to improve government. The committee (or "commission") accordingly approached each of the organizations from which its membership was drawn to request cooperation and financial support. Each of the five agencies involved agreed to provide $3,000 a year for three years beginning in 1946 to secure planning services. In May, 1945, a planning contract was entered into with Harland Bartholomew and Associates, the noted city planning firm of St. Louis, Missouri. A schedule of sixteen projected "chapters" of a planning report for the entire metropolitan area was drawn up with the first four reports to be submitted by October, 1945, and the work to be completed in 1948. By June of 1948, Bartholomew and Associates had presented their reports; these had been reviewed by the committee (and for that matter by the public through widespread publicity and hearings), and were consolidated and refined into *The Master City-Parish Plan.*[13]

The planning activities carried on by this professional organization brought two points forcibly before the public. The first was the inadequacy of existing governmental services and regulation. The general state of affairs is best indicated in the words of the planners themselves when they pointed to the rapid growth of the community and then went on to suggest:

This rapid growth has been occurring without guidance or control.... Any urban area needs streets, sewers, drainage, schools, parks and other facilities. The need for many of these in Baton Rouge has been almost ignored until recently. In comparison with many other cities, Baton Rouge is fully two decades behind in the provision of these essential services and facilities. As a result of this "hit-or-miss" and unplanned growth, we find traffic congestion, substandard dwelling areas, inadequate schools, few parks, an intermixture of land uses, and an urban pattern that has scattered itself far too widely over the land.[14]

The Master City-Parish Plan outlined the government services that urgently required development; These included a metropolitan-wide zoning ordinance and a state law permitting enactment and enforcement of zoning in the parish outside the incorporated area; more stringent subdivision regulations (with minimum standards of streets, sewerage, and water installation before plats were recorded and lots sold); a major street system to overcome the difficulties of disconnected and discontinuous streets and provide new traffic ways; a complete system of schools and parks for all parts of the community; a minimum standard housing ordinance; and the development of a new civic center in the vicinity of the existing courthouse (at the south end of the central business district) which would balance off the state government buildings to the north of the business district. Specific and detailed plans for all of these and related changes were drawn and the master plan generally pointed out that the recommendations could not be carried out in the context of the restricted city limits and the limitations which beset the existing city and parish governments.

Soon after the first reports of Bartholomew and Associates appeared, the committee extended its considerations of the problem of governmental reorganization. Dr. and Mrs. Thomas Reed, well-known consultants on the organization of city government, were brought in to appraise the situation, and arrangements were made with them to undertake a study of overall local government solely from the organizational standpoint. The $10,000 fee for this service was raised by private subscription. On the basis of preliminary study, a proposal for a state constitutional amendment was made. The amendment authorized the creation of a charter commission and enabled that commission to prepare a governmental reorganization plan for submission to the parish electorate within the period 30 to 60 days following the filing of the plan with the parish police jury. The charter commission was allowed a maximum of twelve months to draft the plan. This proposal was approved by the legislature at its regular session of 1946 and ratified in a state-wide referendum at the November, 1946, general election.

The following is a complete text of the constitutional authorization on which the city-parish plan of government is based:

ARTICLE XIV

Section 3 (a) (Added by Act 389 of 1946). The people of East Baton Rouge Parish shall have power to establish, in the manner hereinafter provided, government for the Parish and the several municipal corporations and other political subdivisions and districts situated therein.

(1) There is hereby created in the said Parish a City-Parish Charter Commission consisting of nine persons, who are residents and qualified voters of the parish, three to be appointed by the Police Jury of East Baton Rouge Parish, two of whom shall reside outside the City of Baton Rouge, but within said Parish, two by the Commission Council of the City of Baton Rouge, and one each by the following: East Baton Rouge Parish School Board, Baton Rouge Chamber of Commerce, Director of the Department of Public Works of the State of Louisiana, and the President of Louisiana State University and Agricultural and Mechanical College. Any vacancy in the membership of the commission shall be filled by appointment by the same officer or body who originally appointed the member whose position becomes vacant. It shall be the duty of the said commission to prepare and file with the Police Jury of the Parish of East Baton Rouge within twelve months from the effective date of this amendment a plan for the government of East Baton Rouge Parish and the municipal corporations and other political subdivisions and districts situated therein, provided that if after the twelve months period, the said Commission finds that it is necessary for changes to be made in the constitutional laws of this state before any specific satisfactory plan for the government of East Baton Rouge Parish and the municipal corporations and other political subdivisions and districts situated therein can be worked out and submitted for final approval as above provided, including any changes in the present constitutional enabling provision. In that event the said Commission shall be fully authorized and empowered to prepare and submit to any succeeding session of the Legislature or Constitutional Convention such changes in the constitutional law as the said Commission may deem necessary. It shall be the duty of the said Police Jury to cause the full text of the proposed plan of government to be printed and published within ten days after such filing as a paid advertisement in the official journal of the parish. The question of the adoption of the proposed plan of government shall be submitted at a special election to be held not less than thirty nor more than sixty days from the date of the filing of the proposed plan of government with the Police Jury of the Parish of East Baton Rouge. The said Police Jury shall call and hold such election in the same manner as is provided for the calling and holding of elections on bond issues under Act 46 of the Extraordinary

Session of the Legislature of the State of Louisiana for the year 1921, as amended, except that all qualified voters in the Parish of East Baton Rouge shall be eligible to vote in such election and except that the form of the ballot shall be prescribed by the said City-Parish Charter Commission. The said Police Jury shall promulgate the returns of said elections and shall cause a proces verbal of the election to be filed with the Clerk of Court of said Parish. If the majority of the votes cast at such election are in favor of the proposed plan of government, a certified copy thereof shall be filed with the Secretary of State, and it shall become effective at such time as may be provided therein. A plan of government may be proposed with alternative provisions for submission to the voters for separate vote, and the alternative provisions receiving the larger affirmative vote shall prevail if the plan is adopted.

(2) Subject to the constitution and laws of this state with respect to the powers and functions of local government, as distinguished from structure, organization and particular distribution and redistribution of such powers and functions among the several units of local government within the Parish, such plan of government may provide, among other things:

(a) For consolidation, or reorganization, of all or part of the local governmental units, agencies and subdivisions in the parish, for the elimination or transfer of powers and functions of such units, agencies and subdivisions, for the creation of one or more new local governmental units, agencies and subdivisions, for the reorganization of one or more local governmental units, agencies or subdivisions, for the extension of municipal limits, and for all matters necessary or appropriate to the effectuation of such provisions, including, without limitation, the assumption by one local governmental unit, agency and subdivision of indebtedness of another or other and transfer of official personnel records, funds and other property and assets; and

(b) For revenue for the support of the one or more local governmental units, agencies or subdivisions proposed by the plan, including, without limitation, allocation of parish revenues to other units, agencies or subdivisions.

(3) The plan of government shall provide for the establishment of an industrial area or areas. It shall also provide a method for establishing additional industrial areas by the local government body under the jurisdiction of which such additional industrial area or areas may then or thereafter be situated. No industrial area or areas shall be part of any urban area or urban areas.

An industrial area shall include any compact body of land situated outside the incorporated limits of the City of Baton Rouge at the effective date of this Section 3 (a) and which at the effective date of the plan of government, is used predominantly for industrial purposes, and for which are privately furnished, substantial services normally provided by local governments, and may include other bodies of land so situated and primarily suited for industrial development. Such plan shall also provide for and define rural and urban areas.

The provision of this constitution relating to limitation of taxation by municipalities shall apply in the urban areas and those relating to the limitation of parish taxation shall apply in the industrial and rural areas.

(4) The plan of government shall be subject to amendment by election of the people as provided therein.[15]

In accordance with the foregoing authority, the charter commission worked from November, 1946, until June, 1947, at which time a proposed plan was submitted to the police jury. The basic changes in the existing form of government proposed by the charter commission were the following:

(1) East Baton Rouge would be divided into three areas – rural, urban, and industrial. The urban area, containing the present city and subdivided communities, would constitute the city of Baton Rouge with an area of some thirty square miles instead of the present 4.6 square miles, with an estimated population of 106,000 compared to the present 35,000.[16]

The division into the three types of areas, as indicated, was related primarily to considerations of taxation and was required by the terms of the enabling constitutional provision. The industrial areas (of which more will be said later) were placed outside the corporate limits in order to exempt them from the constitutionally authorized municipal tax (then levied at a seven mill rate, now eight mills). This compromise was made largely at the behest of the industries, who were to be given this exemption from the city taxes in exchange for a commitment to provide their own counterparts to city services – streets, street lighting, sewers and sewerage works, fire and police protection, and refuse collection and disposal. The expansion of the city limits followed the suggestions of Bartholomew and Associates to the effect that an area equal to five times the existing incorporated municipality had undergone urban development to the point of requiring city services.

(2) The entire parish would be governed by a council of nine members, seven of whom would be elected at large from the urban area of the city. The council would select from its own number a parish president, to preside over the council and be the ceremonial head of the city and parish governments, as well as a parish clerk, and a treasurer, which two offices could be combined.

(3) The parish council would select a city-parish manager, who would be a person trained and experienced in public administration, as the chief executive officer of the parish and city. The manager would act also as purchasing agent for the city and parish until and unless the council established such an office.

(4) The City Council would consist of the seven members of the Parish

Council elected from the city and would have authority to adopt the city budget, pass city ordinances and adopt policies relating to the city.[17]

The continued separation of the city and parish governing bodies and the distinction between the city and parish is related in part to tax problems. Parish and municipal tax rates are separately established and a homestead exemption on the first $2,000 of assessed value of owner-occupied residential property is granted in the case of state, parish, and special district property taxes (except for recently created districts). Since municipal taxes are not covered by this exemption, except in New Orleans, the establishment of a parish-wide governing authority might have jeopardized the municipal levy, which was needed for municipal services in the urban area; or contrarily, a merger involving an extension of full-scale municipal police power conceivably could have threatened the homestead exemption privileges. Since the constitution and general laws are geared to a largely separated system of rural and urban governments, adjustments to a number of inflexible legal arrangements had to be made.

A substantial public relations campaign was undertaken to present the plan to the public and to create an atmosphere favorable to its adoption. A governmental information committee of 250 persons was organized, with subcommittees functionally organized to cover major social groups and community interests. Virtually all the civic clubs in the area supported the changes, newspapers and radio carried daily information programs, a series of public hearings evoked much interest, and some twenty thousand posters were utilized during the campaign.

Opposition to the plan was also strong. The objections were fairly typical of those encountered in similar situations. The opposition claimed that taxes would be raised in the areas outside the city, and that Baton Rouge was simply "grabbing up" desirable suburban communities. A second major point of dissent occurred over the creation of industrial zones. Many opponents of the plan saw this as an unwarranted limitation on sources of revenue from industry. Earlier there had been occasional discussion of the idea of incorporating the built-up section of Ward Three (including the industrial area) as a separate municipality. There was a strong sense of community identity in the North Baton Rouge (Istrouma) sector; the Choctaw Road line of demarcation was more than a point of separation between city and suburb – certain hostilities growing out of socio-economic distinctions were present. North Baton Rouge was primarily an industrial employee residential area. In some cases the area's residents were suspicious of the city and regarded an alliance between downtown Baton Rouge civic leaders and industrial management as inimical to their interests. Some opponents of the plan also raised vigorous objections to the adoption of the city manager system, charging that it was "... undemocratic and un-American."[18] Further unfavorable reaction was forthcoming with regard to the election at large of the council members from the City of Baton Rouge and the lack of provision for compensation of council members, because it was felt that these factors would enable only the well-to-do to stand for the council. The pressures were sufficient to cause the charter commission to make some conciliatory changes in the original draft of the plan. Chief among these was the substitution of a popularly elected "mayor-president" for the city manager. A provision for a smaller per diem payment to the members of the council was included, certain changes were made in the proposed city boundaries, and the provision for a parish judge was eliminated, with the result that the city would continue to have an elective city judge and the rural areas would still have justice of the peace courts.

By the time the commission had completed these alterations in late June, 1947, timing had become crucial. In order to meet the constitutional requirement that the proposal be submitted to the voters between 30 and 60 days after the submission of the plan to the police jury, rapid action on the part of the police jury was called for. Opposition from the police jury was substantial, as is attested by the fact that the proposal to submit the plan to the electorate carried by the narrow margin of nine to seven. The election was set for August 12, 1947, which was the last possible date that would meet the time limit established in the constitutional amendment. Even so, objections were raised by opponents of the plan on grounds that insufficient time was available to the voters to permit them to inform themselves about the plan. However, the fact that the issue had been before the public and under discussion for so long before the actual election was called tended to blunt the force of this argument. Dr. Reed also undertook a substantial responsibility for presenting the plan before various groups, and not always friendly groups at that. Of more importance to the success of the plan was the fact that the campaign for it was thoroughly organized and had the advantage of unified leadership, while the opponents, though adamant and outspoken, were far less cohesive and therefore somewhat unsystematic in their opposition. Unified opposition to the plan actually was to become more intense after the proposal was adopted than during the campaign.

The proposed plan of government was popularly adopted by a close vote (7,012 to 6,705) in the parish-wide election of August 12. Despite the importance of the issue, voter turnout was light; less than 50 per cent of the qualified voters cast ballots in all but one ward, only slightly over one-third of those eligible to vote in the

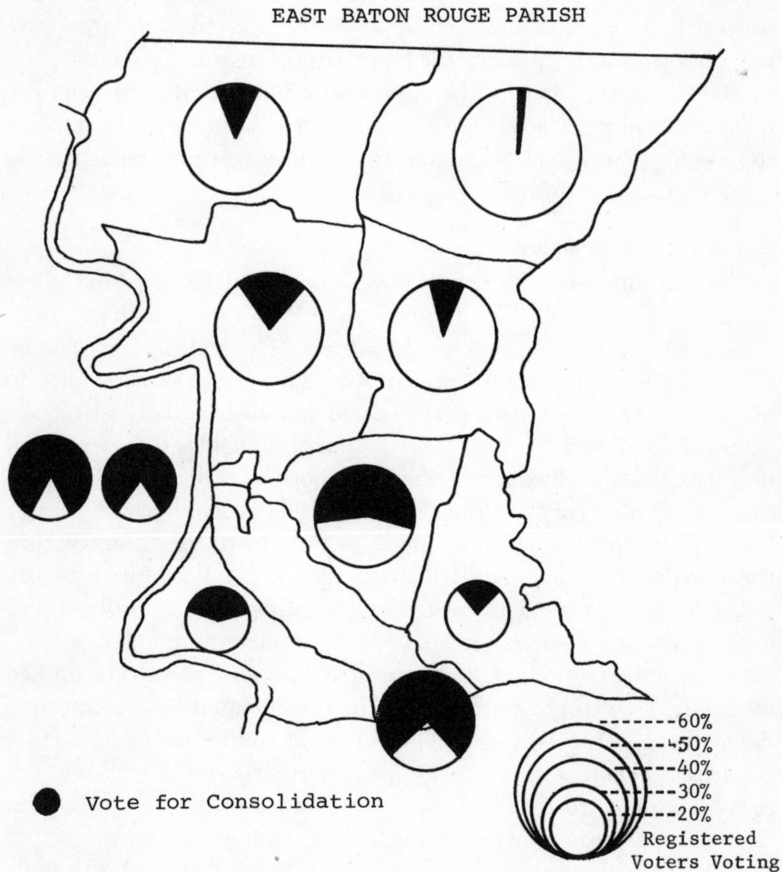

FIGURE IV Votes for Consolidation were Concentrated in the Urbanized Sections of the Parish

city wards participated, and in two wards the ballots cast represented less than 25 per cent of the registered voters. City voters favored the plan almost four to one, two of the wards south and east of the city (six and nine) voted substantially in favor of the plan, and the small and more distant Ward Eight voted against it by a narrow margin. Opposition centered in the wards north of the city, although Ward Seven to the extreme east of the city also delivered a large opposition vote, Figure IV. In Ward Three, the most populous of the northern rural wards, more than 4,000 votes were cast and the distribution of votes was more than three to one against the plan. Although much smaller numbers were involved, the voters in Wards Four, Five, and Ten opposed the plan in even larger proportions. If the frequently used practice of requiring separate approval of such a plan by the rural and city residents had been followed, the plan of government would have been easily rejected in the rural areas, a fact calculated to encourage future opposition in some of those sections of the parish.

The Plan in Summary

The consolidated city-parish government which came into effect for Baton Rouge and East Baton Rouge Parish on January 1, 1949, contained the following general features. The political geography of the parish was extensively altered. The city was expanded to more than six times its former size to include virtually all of the densely populated portion of the parish outside the two small municipalities of Baker and Zachary, both of which continued to exist as separate corporations, Figure V. The new city-parish charter forbade the incorporation of any new city, town, or village within the parish, although special districts could still be created as provided by law. In order to protect outstanding financial obligations, existing special districts were continued under the plan of government, although they would henceforth be more effectively unified under the general government with its consolidated finance and line departments (especially the department of public works).

Three general jurisdictional areas were recognized within the parish, with correlative tax structures and service responsibilities. The City of Baton Rouge, with its expanded boundaries, was vested with the usual municipal powers and service responsibilities; its residents would pay all parish property taxes and would additionally be asssessed the general city levy in order to meet the costs

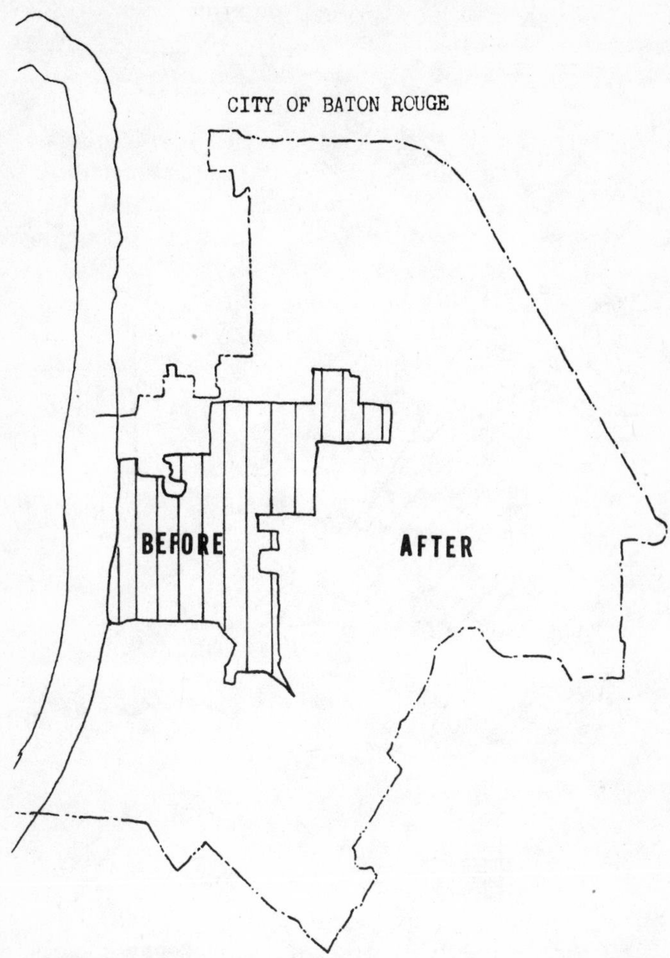

FIGURE V Relative Areas Within Baton Rouge City Limits Before and After Consolidation

of specifically urban services (garbage collection, street lighting, sidewalks, police and fire protection, etc.), which were extended throughout the area embraced by the new city boundaries. The industrial areas (see Figure VI), from which all residential property was to be excluded, were assessed only at the parish rate, on the stipulation that they were to furnish their own services of a municipal type. Failure to maintain these services within the industrial

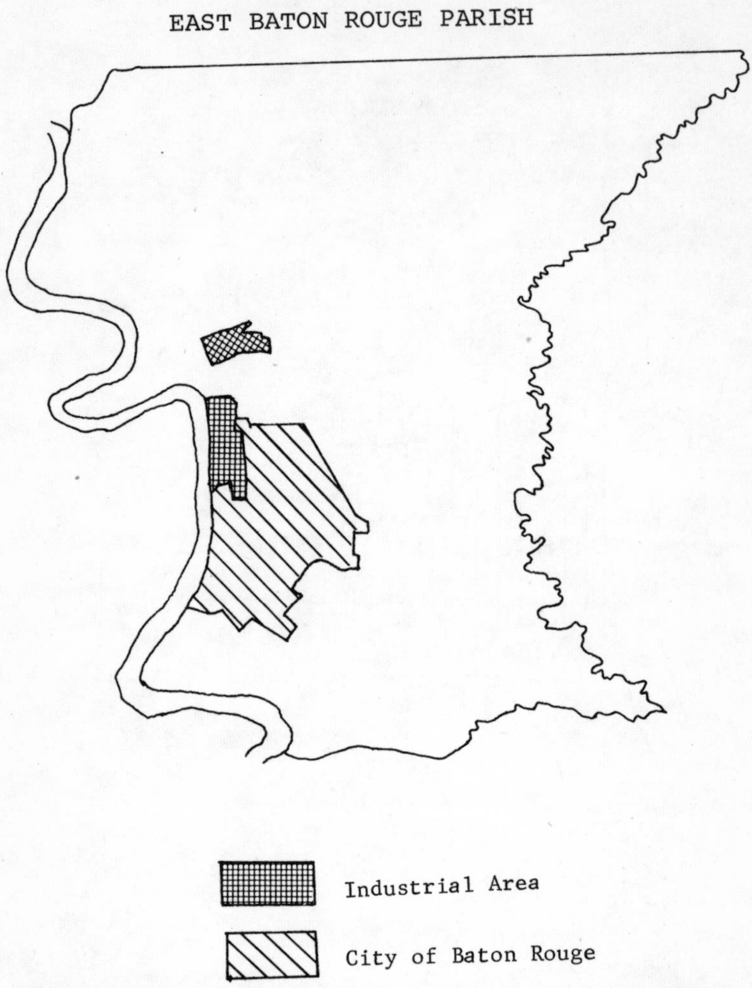

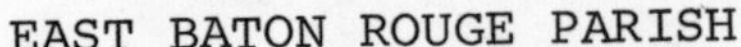

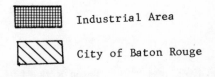

Industrial Area

City of Baton Rouge

FIGURE VI City and Industrial Areas of East Baton Rouge Parish under Consolidated Plan of Government

zone would result in a reversion of the offending sectors to urban status. A portion of the parish general tax in the industrial area was eventually distributed to the three municipalities on the basis of a population formula. The remainder of the parish was to be a rural area, subject to parish taxes and beneficiary of services extended by the general parish government. For electoral purposes Baton Rouge

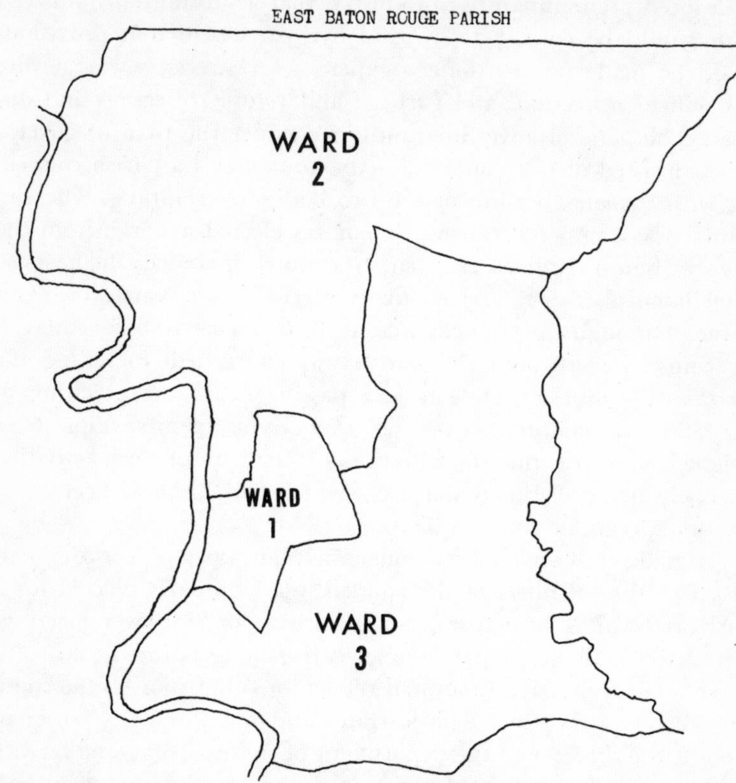

FIGURE VII Ward Divisions of East Baton Rouge Parish After Consolidation

was designated as Ward One, and the rural area was divided into two additional wards, Figure VII.

Special provisions were included for expanding the boundaries of the city and for creating new industrial areas. Municipal annexation depended on the initiative of the area to be annexed; if a majority in number and amount of property taxpayers in a compact body of land adjoining the city (but outside an industrial area) petitioned for annexation, the city council could, after public hearings, annex the territory by ordinance. New industrial areas could be formed out of a compact body of rural area land of not less than 320 acres. Petitions for establishment of these industrial areas were to be filed with the parish council, under the stipulations that the area would be devoted predominantly to industry, that a substantial industrial plant would be constructed within five years, and that provisions would be made (at petitioner's expense) for streets, sewerage, fire and police protection, and garbage and refuse collection and disposal. The general governing authority under the plan of government consisted of two councils, a city council and a parish council, but with the membership of the two bodies overlapping. The city council was composed of seven members elected at large from the City of Baton Rouge; the parish council included these seven councilmen plus two rural members, elected from Wards Two and Three. Although the councils were to function separately insofar as governing the city and the parish was concerned (including the separate adoption of budgets and passing ordinances relating to city and parish functions), the concurrent memberships were designed to assist the coordination of their respective activities, especially in those functional areas which had hitherto been separate and were now to be unified.

The main executive officer under the plan was a mayor-president who, like the members of the council, was popularly elected for a four-year term. The mayor-president was to preside over meetings of both councils, to prepare the executive budgets for the city and parish, and to prepare an annual report for submission to the councils. He was to be chief administrator and was given the power to appoint the director of the department of public works, the finance director, the personnel administrator, the purchasing agent (all largely functionally consolidated for the city and parish), and the municipal fire and police chiefs. The mayor-president or his designated representative was also expected to serve on several boards and commissions. Certain overhead, or staff, functions were consolidated under the plan. Among the more important of these were finance, central purchasing, and personnel administration. The department of finance under the supervision of a director of finance who was appointed by the mayor-president was to assist in budget preparation, provide for a uniform accounting system, and exercise the preaudit function. Centralized purchasing was to be carried out by the division of purchasing headed by a purchasing agent appointed by the mayor-president, and the charter contained provisions which required this office to effect a central property control system. A comprehensive merit system for city and parish employees was outlined in the plan.[19] The administration of this program was to be vested in a personnel director appointed by the mayor-president and a three-member personnel board appointed by the parish council.

Three other consolidated staff offices were to be filled by appointment by the parish council: the attorney, the clerk, and the treasurer. The attorney was assigned responsibility as legal counsel to both councils, to the mayor-president, and to the various departments of the city-parish government. In addition, he was to prepare ordinances and resolutions and to represent the city and parish in litigation in which they might be involved. The clerk, whose office could be combined with that of the treasurer (but was not), was made responsible for city and parish journals, thus establishing his office as the central records office of the two councils. The treasurer was made custodian of all city-parish funds and was responsible for disbursing funds properly certified for expenditure by the director of finance. The organization for consolidated city-parish government is illustrated in Figure VIII.

Of the departments performing line functions, consolidation was most fully effected under the charter in the departments of planning and public works. Since these agencies are treated fully in chapters three and four, only brief mention will be made of them here. The planning function, which is both a staff and a line activity, was a new one for the city and parish. Its administration was vested in a nine-member commission, with provision for a professional staff to work under its direction. The commission was made responsible for both general planning and the preparation of capital improvement programs. In addition, the planning commission was to serve as a zoning commission for the city (and later for the parish when comprehensive zoning was made legally possible). A single department of public works was established under the plan to replace the old parish department under the police jury and the various units of the old city commission concerned with public works activities. Certain divisions of the department were prescribed in the plan of government, apparently in the interest of separating strictly municipal functions (such as garbage collection, sewer maintenance, and inspections) from public works functions that were to be performed over the entire parish. A central garage was established for the service and repair of vehicles and equipment used throughout the parish. One of the more interesting aspects of the consolidation was the fact that Baton Rouge city streets were declared to be parish

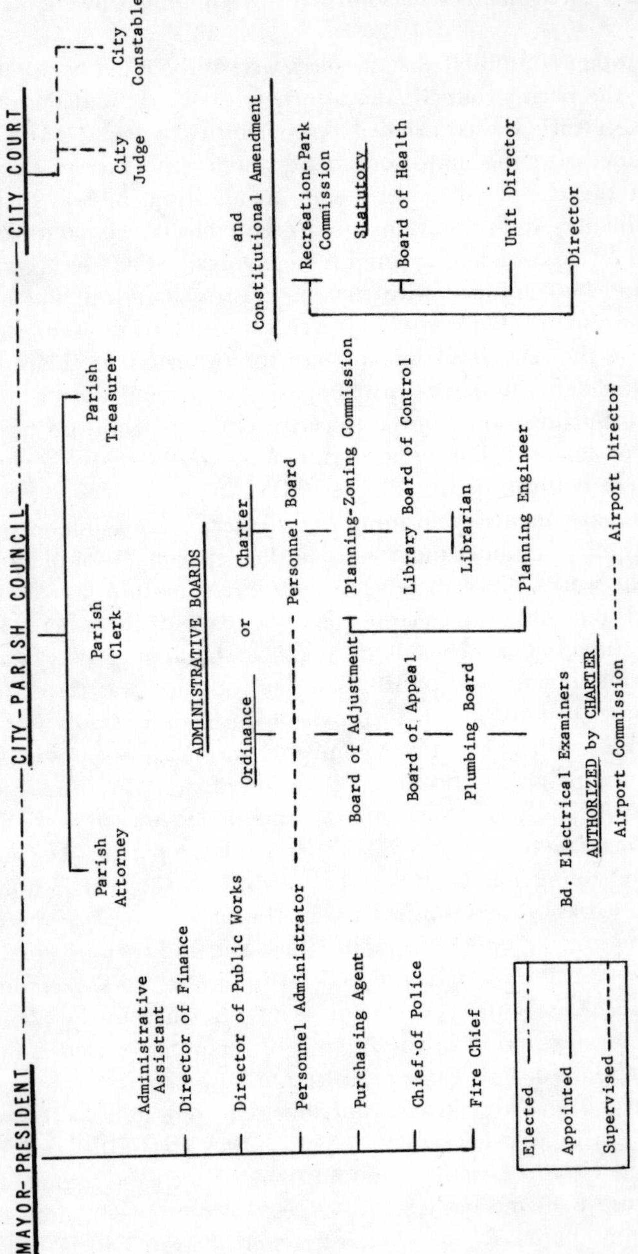

FIGURE VIII Organization of City-Parish Government Resulting from Consolidation

roads. This consolidation of the street and road system offered certain tangible benefits. In addition to unified maintenance under the consolidated department of public works, the change enabled the homestead exemption to be applied against the entire four mills of parish tax;[20] and, since the state reimburses the parishes out of the property tax relief fund for revenues lost to the parishes through this exemption, a considerable financial advantage was realized by this change. Other divisions or costs between city and parish budgets that were affected by provisions in the plan of government are discussed in chapter five.

The remaining functions of government touched upon by the new charter represented continuations of old programs under much the same conditions as previously and are not especially pertinent here. Fire and police departments were included within the sections of the plan applicable to the city; and the recreation and park commission was recognized as a continuing agency of independent status and was authorized to use certain services of the public works department (engineering, building maintenance, and the central garage), the purchasing division, and the personnel system. The parish library was continued and its board was given charter status under the plan; in point of fact, the city was later to include substantial items in its budget to help defray the cost of the library, although technically the library is an institution of the parish. The "constitutional offices" of the old parish government—the sheriff, assessor, clerk of court, and coroner—could not have been abolished without extensive amendment of the state constitution (and for that matter without arousing such political controversy as to endanger plans for consolidation), so they continued to perform their established functions. By the same token, such functions as education, the already consolidated public health activities, and the judicial offices in general were affected only indirectly, if at all, by the change in the local system of government in the Baton Rouge area.[21]

The Plan in Effect

Although the plan of government had been ratified by a narrow popular margin, its success was by no means assured. In addition to the normal transitional problems involved in so substantial a governmental change, the lingering hostility of the adamant opponents of consolidation constituted a threat, as did the possibility that, in the long run and from a practical standpoint, the merger might prove unworkable. As is normal in many jurisdictions, the validity of the new charter had to be adjudicated before the governing authority under it could borrow money or issue bonds. A test suit was accordingly entered by the state's attorney general early in 1949, shortly after the city attempted to issue bonds of indebtedness. The attorney general's brief raised virtually all of the legal arguments that might have been construed as grounds for invalidating the charter, either on procedural or substantive constitutional grounds. The district court, however, upheld the charter against all contesting issues and its decision was affirmed by the state supreme court.[22]

Following the legal validation of the charter, opposition to the plan showed increasing signs of solidification. A series of meetings culminated in the draft of a proposed charter designed to abolish the city government and establish a parish-wide three member commission form of government. This charter, known as the "Webb plan," received its name from the parish assessor, Jesse Webb, Sr., who had emerged as the leader of the unreconciled opposition to the new government. In the fall of 1949, Webb and approximately fifty other opponents of the consolidated plan of government attended a parish council meeting to present a proposal which was held to be a means of effecting a budgetary saving to the parish of some $300,000. Accompanying the Webb charter proposal was a petition requesting that the council call an election on the issue. Since the plan of government contains a clause (sec. 11.09) under which amendments may be proposed upon petition of qualified voters equal in number to 10 per cent of the votes cast for sheriff at the preceding election, the council pledged an amendment election based on the Webb plan. The election was to be carried out despite severe doubts about the constitutionality of the proposal and despite the fact that the names of about 40 per cent of the petitioners had to be removed from the petition because they were not registered voters.

The controversy was intensified when twenty-seven proponents of the charter petitioned the district court for an injunction prohibiting the council's call for an election. The district court permanently enjoined the amendment referendum on the grounds that the proposals violated the state constitution; but when the appeals reached the state supreme court, that body refused to intervene on the grounds that the calling of an election was a legislative function.[23]

In the interim, however, the parish council reversed its previous position and refused to call the amendment referendum, whereupon the opponents of the plan of government sued for a writ of mandamus to force the election. This case, too, followed the now familiar path to the state supreme court where it was finally dismissed on the grounds that the election for sheriff, on which the number of petitioners required to propose an amendment depended, was the primary and not the general election (the difference was that 27,000 votes had been cast in the primary as against 1,000 in the general election) and only 212 registered voters had signed the amendment petition.[24] This action brought an end to the litigation involved in the inception period of the city-parish consolidation.

Approximately two years after the plan of government came into effect, however, it was recognized, both as a matter of concern about the plan and as a result of the pressures of proponents and opponents of the new government, that an objective evaluation of the effectiveness of the new charter was in order. Consequently, the mayor-president proposed, and the parish council adopted, a motion to create a "Plan of Government Study and Recommendation Committee." The eleven-member committee was composed of a mixture of citizen members and officials from the city-parish government. Although Webb was invited to participate and the Independent Taxpayers' Association (largely made up of opponents of the plan from the old Third Ward) was asked to name a representative to the committee, both refused to take part directly. The committee met weekly from late November, 1950, through May, 1951. The committee's deliberations ranged widely, but three general possibilities were considered in detail. One of these was a complete revision of the plan of government in the form of a change to a parish-wide commission form of government. Two proposals were made along these lines: one of them was the "Webb plan"; the other called for a five-man commission for the city, with two additional commissioners from the rural wards. A second set of proposals would have had the effect of amending the charter to restore most of the provisions of the original Reed proposals, including the city-parish manager, which had been struck out of the plan during the course of its development. The third approach, and the one which eventually received greatest support, involved the consideration of a series of amendments which were designed to remedy observable defects in the plan of government.

Toward the close of deliberations, the committee decided to present to the parish council one plan for each type of government—the commission form, the mayor-president and council form (the type already in existence under the plan) with amendments, and the city-parish manager form—with the recommendation that an unofficial ("straw" ballot) election be held so that the people of the parish might express their preference. The plans submitted were those which the committee considered to embody the best features of each of the three types, and were thus not simply the specific proposals brought before the committee by Webb and others. After presentation to the council, the committee's report was turned over to the parish attorney for legal analysis. About a year later, the parish council proposed seven amendments based on some of the changes recommended by the study committee in relation to the existing plan of government. These seven proposals were voted on in July, 1952, and the electorate ratified all but one of them. The defeated proposal, which lost by a narrow margin, would have instituted the most far-reaching change of any of the proposed amendments; it would have had the effect of merging the city and parish councils into a single body, with all members participating in both city and parish decisions, provided the state constitution could be amended to permit this action. The other amendments embodied structural, procedural, and financial changes of less consequence—a change in the distribution of the industrial area's parish tax, alteration in the procedure for passing ordinances and resolutions, an adjustment in the membership of the planning commission, a slight alteration in the membership of the recreation and parks commission, and minor changes in the charter provisions for the city court and city judge, as well as in the office of the city constable.

The study committee did much to alleviate both minor and major objections to the new government: it allowed all parties an opportunity to bring their grievances into the open; the city-parish government was broadly discussed by a prestigious body; some adjusting amendments were made; and public understanding of the rather complex system was enhanced. In fact, the study committee idea was so successful that two other plan of government review committees have been created since that time. The first of these made its report in 1956, and its four proposals for change were subsequently adopted by amendment. These included the addition of the office of administrative assistant to the mayor-president, an increase in the per diem of the council members, provision for a limited veto by the mayor-president, and further alteration of the planning commission's membership. The last review committee sat for eight months in 1959-60 and briefly reconvened in 1961. A number of proposals for change appeared in its report, some of which were put into effect by council or administrative action without the necessity for charter amendment.

At the time of this writing, those committee recommendations that would require charter amendment have not been proposed by the parish council, although these include some substantial recommendations, such as alterations in the personnel system, the absorption of the fire and police civil service by the over-all parish system, some additional qualifications for certain administrative officials in the city-parish government, and the incorporation of the independent recreation and parks commission into the general government of the parish. Several other events further strengthened the position of the newly consolidated government. The adoption of a one per cent city sales tax in 1950 put the experiment on a sound financial basis by enabling services — particularly fire and police — to be extended rapidly to the newly annexed municipal areas and greatly intensified these services in all parts of the city. The surpluses which were reported in the city budget as a result of this step also produced a flexibility in fiscal matters that favorably affected the entire parish. With the election of the late Jesse Webb, Jr. (son of the assessor) as mayor-president in 1952, important dividends were yielded for the new system. The younger Webb had been brought up, and at the time of his election, still lived in old Ward Three, so that much of the opposition from that sector was pacified by his assumption of the highest office of the new government.[25] Furthermore, Webb carried out his administrative duties with vigor and dispatch, whereas the previous (and first) mayor-president had unfortunately suffered a prolonged illness which removed him from active participation in the new government at the very time when energetic executive leadership was greatly needed. A candid appraisal five years after the adoption of the plan of government revealed that the system was effectively in operation and had the tacit, and perhaps the enthusiastic, support of the great bulk of parish residents.

Each of the last two review committees affirmed the increased confidence in the consolidation that came with experience in operating the new government. The 1956 committee indicated that the system was sound and that, because of it, "... the City of Baton Rouge and the Parish of East Baton Rouge are better equipped for the ever increasing problems of a metropolitan area than any other local government in the country." [26] In less extravagant terms, the more recent committee noted that "... this plan appears to be eminently well suited to the efficient and responsible conduct of local government in the area. The Committee is well aware that the future growth and development of this Parish will necessitate adjustments and we believe that the Charter provides an excellent framework within which this development can take place." [27]

In the subsequent chapters we will be concerned to see how well the specific program accomplishments under the city-parish consolidated government warrant these favorable judgments. Special attention will be directed to determining the effects of the plan of government on the parish area outside the city limits.

Chapter III

The Planning Function And Planning Services

Introduction

IN A CONTEMPORARY metropolitan area — especially one in which growth is rapid and geographically expansive — comprehensive planning is not a luxury with which only the affluent community indulges itself. It is a necessity. Within the urbanized part of the metropolitan complex, planning is essential to the provision of the numerous and interrelated municipal services that are a necessary part of large city life. Without thorough analysis of the existing sociological, economic, and physical character of the area and a determination of the service needs and possibilities within it, the orderly provision of these services cannot be effected. The alternative is a haphazard approach to problems in which governmental functions are undertaken or expanded long after the needs for them have come due. Administrative overlapping and functional duplication often occur, and revenues are inefficiently applied. By the same token, the future projection of these considerations, in relation to areas of anticipated development, help to direct growth patterns in the interest of preserving, protecting, and enhancing qualities of the community.

The argument is occasionally offered that professional planning takes decisions out of the hands of local people and places them under the control of a politically nonresponsible bureaucracy. The very opposite is too often the case. Without an acknowledged plan it is difficult to offer the public a choice as to the future of the community; the pressures of special interests move in to fill the vacuum and decisions are reached and implemented without public consideration. A master plan is thus not a fixed and irrevocable substitute for political decisions; it is a guideline which furnishes a comprehensive and rational basis for them. In the actual administration of local government, in a metropolitan area, the planning agency assumes a primary staff role in coordinating the administration of line functions. Planning is an important means of tying diverse, but civically interdependent, activities together. Responsibility for transportation, drainage, provision of sewerage and utilities services, zoning, subdivision regulation, public health, parks and recreation, and public education almost inevitably tends to be dispersed among a variety of specialized administrative agencies. These agencies, in turn, are likely to be acted upon by a multiplicity of interested groups, and to serve different (although sometimes overlapping) clienteles. In the face of this dispersal of influences, a planning agency can be an invaluable instrument for providing the general governmental authority with an overall perspective. In this way each of the activities is appropriately related to the others in striving to subserve general rather than particular objectives and thus to clarify the identity of the community.

Since the primary concern, in the present context, is the nonurban sector of the metropolitan area, it should be emphasized that the planning function is also vital to the residents outside incorporated communities. In the first place, the rural divisions within the boundaries of the metropolitan area are themselves open to urban development. Extension of the planning function of these areas provides not only the major means for assuring that the urban growth will be orderly and accompanied by a projection of necessary public services on as economical a basis as possible, but is also one of the few ways (and often the only way) in which the residents of such areas can participate in the decisions which will determine the nature of their community in the future. And even in those rural sectors in which the possibility of urban sprawl is not imminent, the effects of being immediately adjacent to an urban center (and encompassed by census definition within its sphere) creates planning needs. Some of these needs are direct outgrowths of urbanization, while others are more subtle. As economic interdependence increases, for example, a planned system of access roads is indicated. In addition, the sheer volume of construction of facilities such as roads, industrial plants, residences, etc., may produce changes that call for readjustment on an area-wide basis. Typical of this is the combination of diversion or sealing off of natural drainage channels and causing water to collect in the soil to the point that the existing primary drainage system becomes inadequate.

More indefinite, but nonetheless a phenomenon of increasing interest, is what might be called the "psychological" urbanization of rural residents. The separation between rural and urban ways of life has greatly diminished and in many instances virtually disappeared in terms of household patterns and conveniences, entertainment, shopping habits, and related factors. Such changes, of course, bring with them the demands for many public services similar to those in urban communities, and while these services are in many cases less urgently required in terms of everyday living in rural areas, and are not necessarily as complex as in the case of the municipality, they still require the wisdom of foresight and the techniques of coordination that planning offers.

In terms of services rendered, the planning agency and its functions must justify themselves largely on intangible grounds. Any attempt to indicate the quantitative utility of planning, in dollars and cents terms, will be bogged down in a hopeless mire. Who can estimate the value of anticipating needs and developing services before the ordinary community functions are totally incapacitated by breakdowns in transportation and communications, supersaturation of existing school facilities, damage to persons and property through flooding, impairment of health by substandard housing and inadequate sewerage and water supply? On a lesser scale who can anticipate the extra costs that might accrue to the taxpayer because of inadequate subdivision standards, failure to coordinate major construction so that roads and sidewalks have to be torn up to install sewer lines, or utility installations have to be relocated?

What can be done, however, is to establish as precisely as possible what services the planning agency is actually rendering, and the extent to which the line departments are carrying out their functions under the coordinating influence of the planning agency. The first of these tasks is the main burden of the present chapter; the second is largely reserved for a later one in which the types and extent of services to the rural areas under the city-parish plan of government will be reviewed and their relation to comprehensive planning appraised. Inevitably, however, the present chapter will anticipate the later questions to some extent.

The reader should be reminded at this point that planning was not carried on under the local government pattern which preceded Baton Rouge city-parish consolidation, thus the planning functions cannot be evaluated comparatively except for occasional pre-1949 substitutes for planning. Although planning is a unified operation with unifying objectives, the following discussion breaks the major planning functions into separate parts as a matter of logical convenience.

The Planning Commission and its Functions

A general outline of the organization of the planning commission and its major functions is provided in the *Plan of Government.*[1] The plan establishes a planning commission for the parish (which also serves as the zoning commission for the city)[2] and designates the method of selection of the commission's nine members. Four of the appointments are based on the idea of overcoming the rigid separation of powers; these assignments represent an attempt to intermingle governmental functions and capacities in order to encourage communication and coordination among different agencies. One is a member and appointee of the parish school board, another is a member and appointee of the recreation and parks commission, a third is "... the mayor-president or an officer or employee of the city designated by the mayor-president from time to time"[3] (in practice, this has been the director of public works), and the fourth is appointed by, and from, the parish council. Thus, the commission is linked to the city-parish government in both its legislative and executive branches, as well as to two other largely independent parish-wide administrative agencies.

The remainder of the commission's membership consists of five "qualified voters and taxpayers of East Baton Rouge Parish,"[4] who are appointed by the parish council for terms of five years and serve without pay. Of special interest is the requirement that two of these must be residents of the rural area and three residents in the City of Baton Rouge. In view of the parish's rapid urbanization, the shifting patterns of population, the race to the periphery, and the increasing importance of the suburban-rural area, it is probably useful to have a guarantee of both rural and urban membership in order to have representative spokesmen for the separately identifiable sectors.

The commission elects from its membership a chairman who serves for one year and who is eligible for re-election. It adopts its own rules of procedure and must meet at least once a month. In recent years, it has been necessary to meet regularly twice a month. Usually, planning matters are taken up on the second Monday of each month and zoning business, including public hearings, occupies the fourth Monday. The planning commission is charged by the *Plan of Government* with two primary responsibilities: the aforementioned duty of zoning, and the annual preparation of a program of capital improvements for the ensuing five years. One operating factor which should be noted at the outset, is that the most obvious development in the administrative practices of the commission has been the transfer of technical and administrative tasks to the permanent staff, with a corresponding increase in the number of staff personnel. The planning function has been steadily professionalized as experience in its activities has enlarged. At first the commission itself was heavily involved in actual preparation of plans. As of 1950, there were only two staff members, and the commission utilized six standing committees of its own members.[5] The standing committees have now ceased to function and the staff consists of eight full-time employees. In addition to the planning director, who serves as secretary to the commission, the staff consists of three draftsmen, a planning aid, a secretary, and a clerk stenographer. A planning assistant also serves both in a technical capacity and as a deputy for some of the department's administrative work. The last of the standing committees to relinquish its duties to the staff was the subdivision committee.

After being greatly preoccupied with the development of master plans, especially in the 1955-58 period, the staff was finally able to undertake the subdivision committee's purely administrative responsibility in 1959. Prior to this time the subdivision committee had met twice a month to act in lieu of the whole commission for full and detailed evaluation of proposed subdivisions. Plats are now preliminarily reviewed by the planning director and staff and their recommendations are then brought to the commission in connection with its general review of the proposal.[6] The commission is thus free to devote its efforts to policy and decision making, while details of current and long-range plans are supplied by the staff. The commission, of course, relies on the planning director for advice and for initiation of planning proposals. On the whole, a sensible and practical relationship seems to exist between the professional planner and the commission.

The Demographic Aspects of Planning

One function of the planning commission's staff, which in a sense underlies all others, is constant attention to the growth in parish population and patterns of settlement. The rapid growth which the parish has experienced since consolidation may be illustrated by a comparison of recent census results with the estimates for 1970 made by Bartholomew and Associates in 1948. The Bartholomew report predicted that the 1970 population of the parish would be 157,400, of which 138,000 would reside in the city, with the remaining 19,400 outside of the metropolitan area.[7] The inaccuracy of this forecast can probably be attributed to its reliance on the estimates of the bureau of the census which anticipated that the nation's population would be 157,442,000 by 1970, a figure well surpassed by the mid-1950's. Whatever the cause of its error, the results of the 1960 national census, a 1958 special parish census, and even the 1950 national census proved the Bartholomew projections to be extremely conservative. The earliest of these showed the Bartholomew growth rate estimates to be twenty years behind the facts. In 1950, the population of East Baton Rouge Parish was 158,236, almost one thousand more than the number anticipated for 1970. By 1960, the parish total had risen to 230,058, and after readjustment based on the 1958 special census, the planning commission now expects an additional 100,000 people in the parish by 1970.[8]

The greatest growth has occurred in the rural area of the parish. More specifically, it has occurred in the transitory zone between urban and rural, termed the suburban area by the commission, although according to the *Plan of Government* this suburban fringe is legally a part of the rural area. The population in this band of approximately three miles around the entire northern, eastern, and southern boundaries of the city increased from 20,500 in 1950 to approximately 50,000 in 1959. In the latter year 31 per cent of the total parish population lived in the legally defined rural area, but only 9 per cent of the parish population lived beyond the suburban fringe and 22 per cent was in the built-up area adjacent to the city. Between 1950 and 1959, two-thirds of the total parish growth occurred outside of the city.[9] An elaboration of the rural growth trend on an annual basis from 1948 to June, 1962, is given in Table 1.[10]

By contrast with these figures and the accompanying map showing the accruing need for expanding the municipal corporation and its functions into the suburban area, Tables 2 and 3 show the extent to which annexation has been used to cope with this urban expansion. Although annexations since 1959 are impressive, in comparison with the virtual absence of expansion of the pre-1949 city by this method, one or two factors tend to qualify the initial favorable indication. All of the annexed areas are high quality subdivisions whose residents are aware of the long-range advantages of being inside the city and who want municipal services (for which they paid premium prices while unincorporated); the city, in turn, can regard them as assets rather than liabilities. In addition, while

TABLE 1

Population Data for City of Baton Rouge and East Baton Rouge Parish, 1948-62

Year	City	Rural	Parish Total	Per cent Rural
1948	34,263	113,358	147,621	76.78
1949*	124,091	30,646	154,737	19.80
1950	125,629	32,607	158,236	20.59
1951	127,319	36,268	163,587	22.17
1952	129,060	38,748	167,808	23.09
1953	130,103	40,745	170,848	23.84
1954	132,147	43,534	175,681	24.78
1955	135,547	46,978	182,525	25.73
1956	139,500	52,202	191,702	27.23
1957	143,759	57,580	201,339	28.59
1958	147,357	61,917	209,274	29.58
1959	151,170	70,405	221,575	31.77
1960	152,419	77,639	230,058	33.74
1961	153,856	80,320	234,176	34.29
1962	155,944	84,386	240,330	35.11
1962	156,433	86,959	243,392	35.72

*89,789 people brought into the city as a result of the adoption of the Plan of Government. All estimates are for January 1, except census years. Last 1962 figures are for June.

the geographical size of the annexations is fairly large, it should be recalled that the suburban fringe now directly affects some 30 square miles adjacent to the city. Even allowing for the irregular contours of suburban growth, the density of population has reached

TABLE 2
Subdivisions Annexed to the City of Baton Rouge, 1955-62

Subdivisions	Date Annexed	Area: Acres	Area: Sq. Miles	Population
Broadmoor Area	5/27/59	855.60	1.34	3,447
Jefferson Place	4/22/55	165.30	.26	515
Parkland Place	1/22/58	19.30	.03	205
Glenwood	7/11/56	27.60	.04	72
Palm Hills	7/10/57	11.80	.02	40
Villa Del Ray	8/19/60	573.10	.89	816
Hayes Tract	12/27/61	109.15	.17	--
Meadow Lea	4/14/62	110.80	.17	195
Broadmoor Place	5/11/62	30.92	.05	--
Broadmoor Estates	5/26/62	21.08	.03	--
Totals		1,924.65	3.00	5,290

TABLE 3
Land Areas for Residential Divisions, East Baton Rouge Parish, 1962

Classification	Square Miles	Acres
City	34.96	22,356.51
Rural Suburban	83.74	53,592.93
Rural	350.10	224,080.50
Total Parish	468.80	300,029.94

the point at which overall municipal services are called for in a total area that approximates the size of the existing city. Annexation, then, has not been able to keep pace with the growth of the suburban fringe.

It is obvious from the foregoing tables that since consolidation rural population has steadily been increasing in proportion to the total parish population. From about 20 per cent in 1950 it has grown now to exceed 35 per cent. By 1970, 40 per cent of the parish population is expected to be outside of the city.[11] If so, this would restore the approximate situation that occurred during the 1940's, when 60 to 70 per cent of the parish was rural. Related inferences can be drawn from the population table. While the ratio of city to rural dwellers was 4:1 in 1949, it is now less than 2:1. While the city's population increased 26 per cent from 1949 to the present, and the parish total increased 57 per cent in the same period, the population of the rural area increased 184 per cent, representing a

TABLE 4
Number of Dwelling Units in East Baton Rouge Parish, 1948-62

Year	City	Rural	Parish Total	Per cent Rural
1948	10,125	30,737	40,862	75.22
1949	34,458	7,627	42,805	17.81
1950	37,120	8,817	45,937	19.19
1951	37,491	9,773	47,264	20.67
1952	37,737	10,405	48,142	21.61
1953	37,931	10,903	48,834	22.32
1954	38,415	11,609	50,024	23.20
1955	38,289	12,481	50,770	24.58
1956	40,318	13,821	54,139	25.52
1957	41,429	14,866	56,295	26.41
1958	42,344	16,281	58,625	27.77
1959	43,565	18,450	62,015	29.75
1960	45,785	20,274	66,059	30.69
1961	46,217	21,222	67,439	31.46
1962	46,991	22,956	69,947	32.81
Per cent increase 1949-62	36.37	200.98	63.40	

growth rate which has almost tripled the rate of 13 years ago. The same pattern of growth is further indicated in the annual increase of dwelling units shown in Table 4.[12]

Through 1959 the center of population growth was in the suburban area. A comparison of the percentage of population dispersion of 1959 with that of March, 1962, in the city, suburban, and rural areas reveals that: (1) the city's share of total population has dropped from 69 per cent to 66 per cent; (2) the suburban area fell off slightly from 22 per cent to 21 per cent; and (3) the rural areas showed a 4 per cent increase and now contain 13 per cent of the total parish population.[13] Part of this growth may be accounted for by population increases and geographic expansion in the Zachary and Baker incorporated areas. In other words, not only does population growth continue to be greatest in the constitutionally defined rural area, but it is becoming greatest in the designated rural area. While both the city and noncorporate areas are increasing in numbers, *proportionally,* the city is declining in importance, the suburban-rural areas are relatively stable, and the rural-rural area is gaining. Even if various factors, including the interstate highway, the consolidated sewer district, and business and civic efforts to revitalize the central business district may retard this centrifugal trend, it is nevertheless possible that dispersal will continue to the point at which virtually the entire parish will eventually be urbanized. Even the slow-down of industrial development in the parish has not affected the situation very much since industrialization has proceeded apace in the adjacent parishes to the south, while the accompanying residential growth has been in the Baton Rouge metropolitan complex. Should the rural-rural growth trend be arrested, it is expected that the primary center of growth would revert to the suburban area.[14]

Numerous questions of interest, possibly of controversy, are raised by the changing character of the parish's demography. Is it time, for example, to consider a major annexation similar to the one of 1949? The planning commission's first director suggests strongly that it is. Or, as an alternative, should the parish tax base be readjusted commensurate with the new areas of population growth and governmental activity? A related problem which already intrudes itself is that of representation by population. The urban-rural conflict now harassing some state legislatures is developing in reverse, in terms of the urban-rural composition of the parish council. Immediately after annexation and consolidation the two rural councilmen represented less than 20 per cent of the parish total, which was then a fair apportionment. By 1962, however, the two rural councilmen represent more than 35 per cent of the parish populace. Expressed in constituents per councilman, alterations of the original scheme of representation is more striking. In 1949, each city councilman represented 17,727 people while each rural delegate averaged 15,313 constituents. As of June, 1962, however, each city councilman was representing 22,347 and each rural councilman 43,479. The latter figure is also an average, because in fact the Ward Two councilman represents more than 50,000 residents. Continuous demographic analysis by the planning staff is a necessary precursor of all of the other planning functions because population trends are the indicators of future needs for zoning, subdivision control, and the installment of facilities such as roads, schools, utilities, and drainage and sewerage systems. The orderly implementation of local services which the city-parish form of government was designed to achieve has depended in no small part on the development of comprehensive planning, in which demographic projection was a first priority.

Zoning

Rural land use was not regulated in East Baton Rouge Parish until October of 1958. When the *Plan of Government* was adopted eleven years earlier, its authors had been thoroughly aware that state law did not permit zoning activities to extend beyond the limits of municipalities. Consequently, the planning commission's capacity as a zoning agency was temporarily restricted to the land area within the City of Baton Rouge. However, the *Plan of Government,* with commendable foresight, stated that "if the Parish of East Baton Rouge is authorized to zone property outside of incorporated municipalities, the Planning Commission, in its capacity as the Parish Planning Commission, shall constitute the Zoning Commission provided for by such laws." [15] Special authority to permit parish-wide zoning in East Baton Rouge Parish was extended by

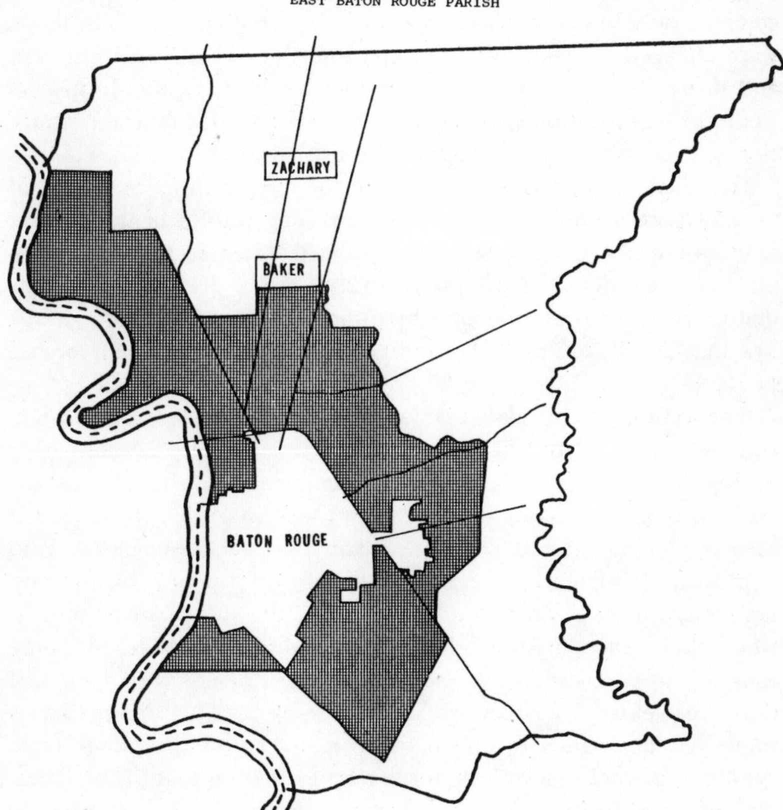

FIGURE IX Shaded Area Shows Extent of Zoning Beyond City Limits of Baton Rouge in March, 1962

Act 409 of the 1956 legislative session. In deference to the *Plan of Government,* sec. 6 of the act provided that the planning commission should act as the zoning commission for the parish. For almost three years following the state grant of authority in Act 409 of 1956, the planning commission worked toward developing a parish zoning ordinance. Preliminary efforts had begun prior to the passage of the state enabling act, however, for in January, 1956, the parish planning commission had launched a comprehensive land use and zoning study.

The need for parish-wide land use regulation was seen immediately. Some funds for this purpose were provided through the Urban Planning Assistance Program of the Housing and Home Finance Agency. These funds were matched by $15,000 from the commission's budget; in consequence, expert planning consultants were engaged to assist in the preparation of a parish zoning map and ordinance. Land use data supplied by the City and Industrial Planners Corporation's survey of 1956 were mapped by the commission and analyzed by Bartholomew and Associates in 1957. The two latter organizations collaborated on the preparation of the final proposed map and ordinance, and in 1958 public hearings were held as part of the review of the project. After 42 planning commission meetings and 12 public hearings on parish zoning, the matter then went to the parish council, which after more public hearings, finally adopted the zoning ordinance and map in October of 1958.[16]

The result of the elaborate and impressive undertaking ostensibly was zoning for the entire parish, but actually amounted to zoning only for the city and suburban area. In other words, the city was rezoned (having initially been zoned in 1950), the suburban area bordering the city was zoned, and the remaining parish land area was left virtually without the benefit of land use regulations, Figure IX. While zoning did not cease at the suburban boundary, since all of the parish land area was technically zoned by being assigned to a classified use, effective zoning did not then, and still does not, extend beyond the suburban area. The distinction is somewhat analogous to one between *de jure* zoning and *de facto* zoning, the areal space of the former far exceeding that of the latter. The great majority of the suburban area is zoned A-1, single family dwellings. This sector's requirements are by far the most restrictive, requiring 10,500 square feet of land per family. To the north of the city, a relatively small portion of the suburban area, perhaps less than 10 per cent of the total, is zoned A-2, single family, and A-3, limited residential. The former requires smaller lot areas than A-1 and permits garage apartments while the latter requires smaller lot areas than A-2 and permits multiple unit dwellings and row housing. In this same general area, located to the west of Ryan Airport, is a light industrial district, Figure X.

A limited industrial district bordering the Illinois Central Railroad's approach to the city from the east divides the suburban area north and south. Almost all of the suburban area to the south is A-1, with the exception of two strip-type commercial developments, one along Hammond Highway and the other along the Airline Highway. Scattered throughout the A-1 district, north and south, are smaller, more localized commercial districts of various types. The intent of the originally proposed zoning map,[17] based upon the Bartholomew report, "How Much Commercial Area Should be Zoned in Suburban Districts," was to discourage strip commercial zoning and to provide, instead, commercial areas suitable for development as neighborhood-type shopping centers.[18] However, concessions to discontent with this plan (as expressed at public hearings), and subsequent piecemeal rezoning have combined to produce commercial strip zoning along several major access thoroughfares. Outside of the suburban area, the remainder of the area defined as rural by the *Plan of Government* is zoned "rural district." The designation implies more of a location than a regulation of land use. The zoning ordinance[19] permits any use of land in the rural district, with a few enumerated exceptions. The exceptions are junk yards, auto salvage or scrap yards, slaughter houses, canneries for fish and meat products, and any use "which may be obnoxious because of smoke, dust, odor, or vibration." [20] Nothing in the ordinance restricts the use of land in the rural district to agricultural purposes. Lot sizes are governed by the city-parish subdivision ordinance, which calls for 20,000 square feet of area unless a sewer collection system is provided, in which case a minimum area of 6,000 square feet is permitted.

Since adoption of the parish-wide zoning ordinance, the annual rate of rezoning requests has tripled as compared to the period prior to 1958, when only the city was zoned. However, since slightly less than a third of the rezoning cases have concerned property outside the city, it can be said that extension of land use regulations to the

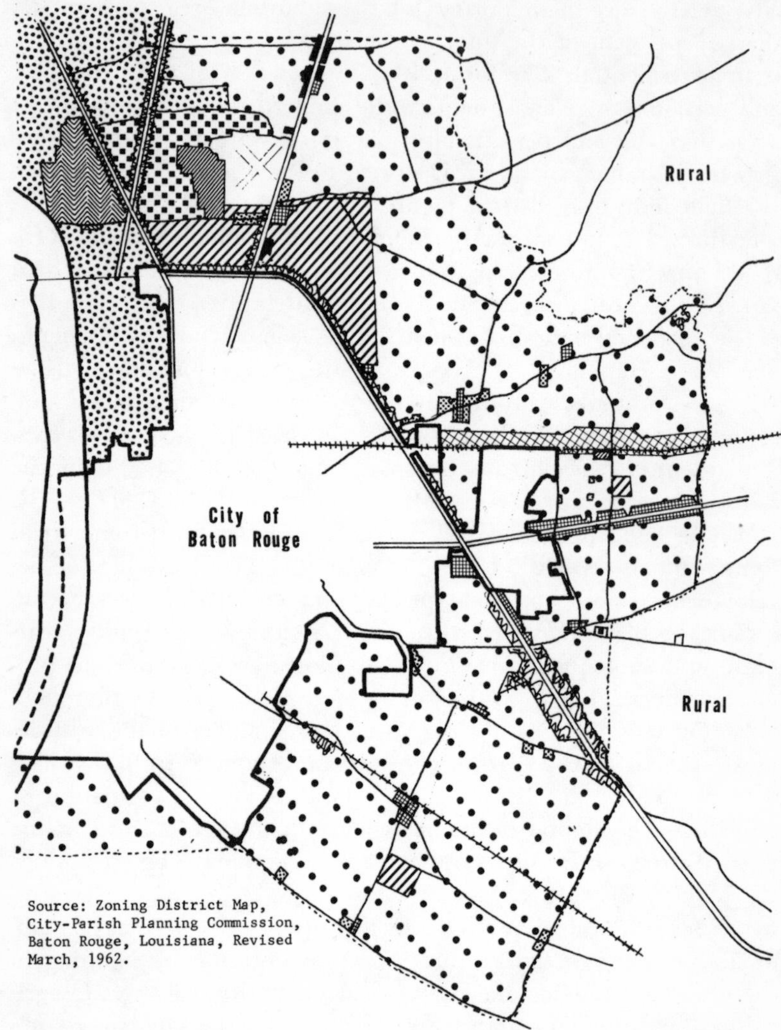

FIGURE X Nature and Extent of Zoning Beyond the Baton Rouge City Limits

rural area affected the increased rate mainly in an indirect manner. i.e., through an increased public awareness of the zoning process which was fostered by public hearings on parish-wide zoning.[21] It is possible to conjecture — although no more than this at present — that the introduction of parish-wide zoning has had the effect of

USE	DISTRICT and SYMBOL	FRONT-SIDE-REAR YARDS	LOT WIDTH	LOT AREA
		ft.	ft.	sq. ft.
SINGLE FAMILY Single family dwellings, churches, schools, and institutions. (on 10 acre sites)	A-1	30' - 8' - 35'	75'	10,500
SINGLE FAMILY Uses permitted in "A-1" district. Garage apartments.	A-2	25' - 5' - 30'	60'	7,500
LIMITED RESIDENTIAL Uses permitted in "A-1" district. Two, three, and four family dwellings, (row housing).	A-3	20' - 5' - 25'	50'	6,000
GENERAL RESIDENTIAL Uses permitted in "A-3" district, multiple dwellings, hospitals, institutions, clubs.	A-4	20' - 5' - 25'	50'	4,000
LOCAL COMMERCIAL Uses permitted in "A-4" district, office buildings, studios, parking lots, retail stores, service stations, radio and T.V. repair, banks.	C-1	25' -None- 20'	50'	None
COMMERCIAL Uses permitted in "C-1" district, drive-ins, garages, hotels, motels, auto repair, car sales.	C-2	None-None-None	50'	None
COMMERCIAL Uses permitted in "C-2" district, and trailer parks.	C-3	None- 50' - 50' or 10%	75'	None
HIGHWAY COMMERCIAL Uses permitted in "C-3" district, laundries, bakeries, bottling works.	C-4	None- 50' - 25'	75'	None
LIGHT INDUSTRIAL Any use not obnoxious due to emission of odor, dust, noise, gas, or vibration.	M-1	None- 25' -None	None	None
LIMITED INDUSTRIAL Same as "M-1" district.	M-2	None- 50' - 30' or 10%	100'	None
GENERAL INDUSTRIAL Any use except residences.	M-3	None- 25' -None	None	Residences not permitted.

Code explanation for Figure X

narrowing the previously unhampered possibilities for subdivision developers and other prospective builders outside the city, thus forcing them to reconsider the prospects for land utilization within the city. Under the parish zoning ordinance annual average requests for rezoning in the city have doubled as compared to practice

TABLE 5

City and Parish Rezoning Actions, Baton Rouge, 1958-61

Action Taken	City	Parish	Total	Per cent of Total
Zoning Commission				
Recommended	131	52	183	68
Denied	61	27	88	32
Total	192	79	271	100
Council				
Approved	141	61	202	75
Denied	51	18	69	25
Total	192	79	271	100
Per cent of total	71	29	100	

under the city zoning ordinance. Table 5 summarizes rezoning actions for 1958-61.[22]

Although Table 5 does not indicate it, no requests for rezoning were received from the rural district beyond the suburban fringe; all parish requests concerned lands in the suburban area. Two possible explanations may account for the absence of requests for rezoning in the rural district. One is a lack of general activity involving changes in land use in that area; the other relates to the previous suggestion that no effective zoning exists in the rural district. Inasmuch as the proportional increase in population since 1958 has been greatest in the rural district, it appears that the latter explanation carries greater weight. Because virtually no restrictions exist in the agricultural zone, development is largely open to whatever uses the new builder may desire. Where rezoning has taken place, that is, in the city and suburban area, actual changes in land usage have taken place in only a fraction of the cases in which requests were approved. As of January, 1961, only 25 of the 147 rezoning requests approved since 1958 have actually resulted in changed usage. Of these, seven changes of 46 approvals have taken place outside the city and 18 (of 101) within the city. The planning and zoning commission concludes that "the majority of the map changes are speculative, rather than being based upon the reasonableness of the zoning prior to the map change." [23]

In summary, zoning is relatively new in application to the rural area. Much to the credit of the *Plan of Government,* zoning follows a uniform set of regulations for both city and rural areas, and the zoning ordinance is uniformly administered by a consolidated planning commission and a consolidated council. In effect, the *Plan of*

Government created a parish zoning commission before parish-wide land use regulation was permitted, thus allowing the greatest possible speed of application by an experienced agency when the state acted to permit parish zoning. In consequence, zoning in the suburban part of the rural area is comparable to that in the city. The remainder of the unincorporated portion of the parish is at least assigned to a category of land use regulation (unrestrictive and loose though it may be), whereas earlier even this possibility did not exist. With the opportunity afforded by state legislation, and through the agency provided by the *Plan of Government,* zoning for the total rural area can be readily achieved as soon as its justification becomes obvious. In the meantime, suburban zoning is transitional zoning. The planning commission, in its report to the Housing and Home Finance Agency, commented on zoning for the rural area as follows:

> It is felt that the Rural Area is still too sparsely developed to require the type of zoning proposed for the Suburban Area, but it is also recognized that further study and land use classification is required in the immediate future as soon as the zoning is established in order to accomplish the aims and principles of Parish-wide zoning.[24]

Subdivisions

Until 1959, the single most time-consuming activity of the planning commission staff was regulation of new subdivision developments. Since 1959, a general slowdown in subdivision activity has been apparent. In 1961 a further decline[25] in the construction trade and a corresponding diminution in this phase of the planning function was evidenced; subdivisions, nevertheless, still demand much of the staff's attention. The overwhelming majority of subdivision development continues to be in the rural area. Since this is the case, the regulation of subdivision activity by the planning commission will probably prove to be of more long-range benefit to the rural area than to the city.

A city subdivision ordinance was adopted in 1949, and in 1955, a consolidated city-parish subdivision ordinance was put into effect. During the six-year interim, regulation of the subdivision of land in the parish was governed by the police jury ordinance of October 10, 1944, in accordance with an opinion prepared by an assistant parish attorney when the question arose in 1950.[26] Although this ordinance was in force before the *Plan of Government* was inaugurated, its enforcement by the planning commission was more stringent than its earlier administration through the police jury. The latter body, having no professional assistance and being especially subject to the cross fires of local pressures, tended to devote more time to requests relating to the section on "variations and exceptions" than to the development and enforcement of uniform requirements.[27] Even if these administrative deficiencies are left aside, a summary comparison of the police jury ordinance and the city-parish subdivision ordinance reveals the superiority of the present set of regulations over the earlier parish code. The recently adopted code provides more stringent requirements of the subdivider in matters relating to streets and sidewalks, sewerage and sanitary standards, drainage, and dedicated lands. One of the more prominent advances made by the new ordinance was the extent to which its requirements were related to other governmental functions.

Mention has previously been made of the relationship between the subdivision ordinance and the location of schools, which is heavily dependent on the ordinance requirement that subdividers reserve sites for public uses. The ordinance also extends city standard street requirements to the suburban area within the boundaries of the consolidated sewer district, with the result that practically all subdivision developments in the rural sector designated as "suburban" are now required to have complete curbing, guttering, and storm drainage.[28] In addition, the ordinance takes full cognizance of the master plan for parish streets and roads. In cases in which a subdivider plans a development which surrounds an existing or proposed major street or road or is adjacent to it, the planning commission can require higher street standards than would otherwise be necessary.[29] Such subdivision activity indicates that overall planning since consolidation has gone beyond concerns of the immediate locale and is carried out with due consideration of the many factors which have a bearing on the development of the entire parish. Table 6 gives an indication of the importance of subdivision regulation to the rural area of the parish in terms of sheer volume. In this respect, the planning commission has provided valuable service in meeting the increasing challenges presented by the areas outside the city limits.

Master Plan for Parish Roads

On April 17, 1950, the Citizens Advisory Committee on Major

TABLE 6
Rural Subdivisions Approved for Development, East Baton Rouge Parish, 1953-61

	Subdivisions			Lots Provided		
Year	Total	Rural	Per cent Rural	Parish Total	Rural	Per cent Rural
1953	207	166	80	---	---	---
1954	339	300	88	4,729	3,908	83
1955	142	101	71	8,120	6,867	85
1956	126	102	81	8,487	8,021	95
1957	99	82	83	7,160	6,919	97
1958	125	99	79	10,645	9,654	91
1959	97	81	84	6,849	6,272	92
1960	78	66	84	4,512	4,134	92
1961	28	24	86	1,249	1,141	91

Streets submitted its recommendations to the planning commission for a master street plan for the City of Baton Rouge.[30] The citizens group had been requested by the commission to "recommend a major street plan, i.e., which streets in the city are to be considered in the major street network," [31] but no similar advice was solicited for the development of a master plan for parish roads. Nevertheless, a master road plan was adopted on June 19, 1950, at the same meeting of the planning commission at which the master city street plan was adopted.[32] The commission attached primary importance to the master street plan (city) and relegated minor considerations to the major road (parish) plan.[33] For example, when the planning engineer advised the adoption of the advisory committee's street plan with only minor modifications, he added that "some Major Road plan for the Parish should also be adopted prior to the adoption of parish subdivision regulations by the Planning Commission." [34] Obviously he did not consider the need for parish subdivision regulations imminent because "he suggested that this parish road plan might consist of state maintained roads within the Parish, which plan would be subject to restudy at a later date." [35]

Public hearings (as required by law) on the street and road plans were held simultaneously.[36] In resolving to hold the hearings the commission directed the planning engineer to advertise the hearings properly, including publication of the map of the proposed street plan for the city.[37] However, he was not directed to publish a map of the parish road plan, and at the hearing, little attention was devoted to it.[38] In other words, the hearing, in effect, was for the purpose of compromising the issues centering about the adoption of a master street plan and at the same time placing a rubber stamp of approval on the noncontroversial major road plan. Nevertheless, having satisfied legal requirements, the major road plan was officially and unanimously adopted by the commission on June 19, 1950. The plan was essentially nothing more than that suggested by the planning engineer; namely, the state highway network as it then existed within the parish. The actions that occurred relative to the major street and road plans in this early adaptation to the *Plan of Government* do not necessarily reflect neglect of the problems of rural constituents of the city-parish government. They point rather to the urgency of the needs of through streets and arterial connections within the built-up area which was now almost entirely within the city limits. In no small part, the needs had arisen from the disabilities which prevented all planning and virtually precluded administrative coordination under the separate city and parish governments. The twenty-five square miles of suburban development newly incorporated into the city and potential access to the adjacent industrial zones were the major sources of street and transportation difficulties. The difficulties resulted precisely from the fact that the city streets and suburban streets had not previously been coordinated. The city street plan was carefully proposed, modified, and adopted, and the parish road plan was merely a title designed to give parish-planning "status" to a segment of the state highway map.[39] To this extent the planning commission gave advance recognition to the future needs of the rural area of East Baton Rouge Parish.

The overriding purpose of adopting both a parish road and city street plan at the same time, rather than a street plan alone, was based on the idea that "these plans were to be used as a guide post for zoning and subdivision ordinances." [40] The extension of the city limits in 1949, which enlarged the city area to approximately six times its former size and increased the population by 89,789 people overnight,[41] brought into Baton Rouge the major sectors of population growth and immediately foreseeable areas of subdivision development. The extension was designed to encompass completely the urbanized area of the parish.[42] The rural area of the parish was not then in such dire need of extensive preliminary subdivision and zoning regulations as was the corporate area. Furthermore, since the commission had no legal authority to zone in the parish outside the city limits,[43] it was less important to outline a detailed road system to support the immediate zoning function than it was to anticipate the possibilities of the future. The first real step in the direction of a comprehensive parish road plan was taken in 1956 when the need arose to lay the groundwork for a parish zoning ordinance. In the fall of that year, after seven years of experiment and experience with planning under the still new form of government, the second master plan for parish roads and streets was adopted by the commission. Thus, although actual planning of rural roads did not take place until some six years after the consolidation of the city and parish governments, the unique city-parish form of metropolitan government furnished a flexible basis for this service to the rural area when its need became obvious.[44]

The plan was obviously the first real plan for roads in the parish and it was also the first attempt to consolidate the parish road plan with the older major street plan which had been "amended periodically to keep pace with growth and change in the City."[45] The new plan, like the earlier street plan, was to provide "subdivision guidance" and a "framework for zoning."[46] Unlike its predecessors, the second plan placed greatest emphasis on the area outside of the city.[47] It declared the existing major street plan to be "an integral part" of the parish road system and urged the development of a "comprehensive system of Parish Roads in time to serve our needs."[48] The system proposed by the commission was designed to facilitate free movement of large volumes of traffic throughout the entire parish.[49] It not only was to make easier the flow of rural-urban traffic, but, more important, it envisioned long-needed major road systems which would be within and for the rural area.[50]

The population of the city had increased only 12 per cent from 1949 to 1955 while the rural area had grown at almost six times this rate. There was a definite need to accommodate the transportation requirements of this growth by development of an extensive system of major roads. The new master plan for parish streets and roads accordingly designated an increased number of roads in the parish as "major" roads and anticipated the acquisition of wider rights-of-way and additional paving to provide an integrated road system in the rural area. In contrast to the former "major" road plan, many of these roads were parish roads rather than state highways.

The major roads of the parish under the new master plan were to be of four types: (1) radial, or those roads radiating from the city; (2) belt roads, or those roads crossing the radials in wide arcs at different distances from the central business district; (3) connectors, or neighborhood roads usually following a horseshoe shaped path and crossing both a radial and a belt; and (4) interparish roads, which connect roads in adjoining parishes and radials within the parish.[51] All but the connector roads are shown on the accompanying map, Figure XI. All four types of roads require 100-foot rights-of-way "except where lighter traffic is anticipated."[52] The plan called for initial paving of two-lane highways (open-ditch roads), with later development extended to four lanes in a number of cases. Table 7 indicates the new road construction in the parish

TABLE 7
Summary of Parish Road Plan, 1948

Type of Roads	Length	Needs Right of Way (Miles)	Needs Paving
Belts	73.9	24.1	29.4
Radials	134.1	7.4	13.3
Inter-parish	67.9	9.9	32.1
Connectors	132.6	48.7	33.9
By-Pass	17.9	---	---
Total System	426.4	90.1	108.7

envisaged as part of the master road plan.[53] It is difficult to determine how much of the major road plan actually has been completed.[54] No running, periodic account of the development of the master plan has been kept by either the planning commission or the department of public works. Furthermore, major road work has been carried out beyond that outlined on the master plan, and segments of the major road plan have been developed by organizations other than the city-parish government. Improvements have been made by the state highway department on some state highways that are part of the road system embraced by the plan; subdividers have had to assume responsibility for others. In the absence of progress reports on the periodic status of the master plan for

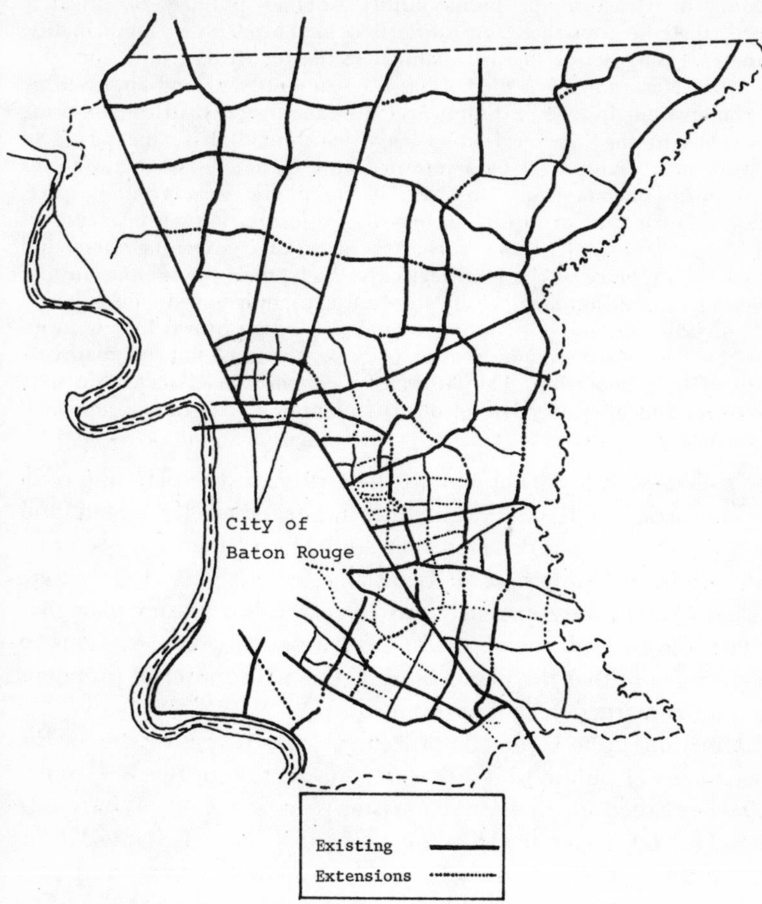

FIGURE XI Master Road Plan for East Baton Rouge Parish, 1956

major streets and roads, it is difficult to evaluate the success of the plan by simply comparing the road systems of 1956 and 1962. Despite these complexities one observation can be made: the parish council clearly has *not* adhered to the master plan for major streets and roads. In this regard, attention is directed to Louisiana Revised Statute 33:109, entitled "Legal Status of Official Plan":

Whenever a commission has adopted a master plan of a parish or municipality, as the case may be, or one or more major sections or districts thereof and has filed certified copies thereof as provided in R.S. 33:108, no street, square, park or other public way, ground, or open space, or public building or structure, or public utility whether publicly or privately owned, shall be constructed or authorized in the parish or municipality, as the case may be, or in such planned section or district until the location, character and extent thereof has been submitted to and approved by the commission. In case of disapproval the commission shall communicate its reasons to the local legislative body, which shall have the power to overrule such disapproval by a recorded vote of not less than two-thirds of its entire membership. However, if the public way, ground, space, building, structure, or utility is one the authorization of financing of which does not under law or charter provisions governing same, fall within the province of the local legislative body, then the submission to a planning commission shall be by the board, commission, or body having such jurisdiction, and a planning commission's disapproval may be overruled by said board, commission, or body by a vote of not less than two-thirds of its membership. The failure of a commission to act within sixty days from and after the date of official submission to a commission shall be deemed approval.

One source of R.S. 33.109 is Act 319 of 1946. In the planning commission's resolution establishing the master plan for streets and roads the commission declared that "this Master Plan has been prepared under the provisions of Louisiana Act No. 319." [55] The commission's intention apparently was to establish a master plan that would take full advantage of the legal restraints on deviations in order to assure that the plan would be the main source of proposals for road construction or improvement.

Extractions from capital improvement reports and reports of the department of public works, however, reveal that of the 108.7 miles of paving called for by the 1956 master plan (see Table 7) only 23.7 miles had been completed as of 1961, at a cost of $1,286,525.22. During this period a total of 34.0 miles of parish roads were paved from capital improvement funds at a cost of $1,803,660.02.[56] The master road plan is thus a long way from complete realization in terms of minimum needs established in 1956. If the present rate is continued, it will be 1980 before the parish road plan's basic paving requirements are met. On the other hand, in the five-year period following the adoption of the master road plan, the parish council authorized the paving of 10.3 miles of parish roads which are not in the master plan. If this work had been applied toward the roads in the master plan, and if that rate of development were to continue, the completion date of the plan would be almost ten years sooner than can now be expected. These actions of the council, which accounted for one-third of capital improvement funds expended for parish road construction, were apparently taken without going through the processes implied in the master plan and prescribed by R.S. 33:109. The council could have submitted its request to the commission for approval of the ten miles of road work, and could have overridden the commission were its requests denied; instead it seems to have acted independently.

Since the plan of government grants the planning commission "all the powers and duties conferred or imposed on parish planning commissions by the general laws of the state,"[57] it can be logically inferred that the object of the charter was to assure that major road construction would be undertaken almost exclusively as a product of professional planning. In deviating from the master plan so substantially, it is likely that the parish councilmen were fulfilling commitments made prior to the adoption of the plan.[58] At the same time, the commission has been reluctant to press its legal position for fear of destroying the excellent rapport now existing between the city-parish planners and the council, and public support of the master plan has not been great enough to demand absolute conformity to it.

On the positive side, two-thirds of the road projects approved by the parish council have been in conformity with the master plan. Furthermore, the council has requested, from time to time, that certain roads under consideration for major improvements be placed on the master plan; and when such proposed inclusions have been denied by the planning commission, the council has refused to carry out its proposed project, often in the face of political and public pressure. If conformity to planning decisions in major road location and development is the ony criterion of the effectiveness of rural planning services in the field of highway transportation, the record under the plan of government is somewhat spotty. Comparison with the total lack of planning of intraparish road projects and the narrow geographic confinement of the areas within which road development decisions were made under the previous form of local government leads to the conclusion that substantial gains have been made in preparing the way for convenient motorized access of rural residents to places of employment, to markets, to governmental headquarters, and to recreation facilities. These new road planning services have finally been coordinated with the planning of other services of local government.

Schools

The planning commission has rendered a notable service to the area under study by assisting in the selection of parish school sites. The new government structure was definitely designed to promote cooperation between the school board and the planning commission. It was outlined in the plan of government that one of the commissioners "shall be a member of the school board for a term coincident with his term on the school board."[59] With this stipulation, the foundation was laid for subsequent developments which allowed the planning commission to influence, and in many cases to be the primary agency in determining the location of schools in the rural area of the parish, as well is in the city. One of the first steps toward implementing the idea of coordinating school administration and planning services was the adoption of the city-parish subdivision ordinance in 1955. The old parish subdivision ordinance contained no provision relative to the location of schools, consequently, when its administration was undertaken by the planning commission in 1949, that body was limited in its attempts to influence the location of schools in the rural area. To alleviate this situation, section VII of the 1955 city-parish subdivision ordinance was included to provide for planning aid to school authorities.[60]

> Parks, Playgrounds, School Sites, etc. In subdividing property, consideration shall be given by the development to the dedication or reservation of suitable sites for schools, parks, playgrounds, and other areas for public use so as to conform to the recommendations of the (planning) Commission in its adopted master plan or portion thereof of the City and Parish. Areas to be dedicated or reserved for schools, parks and playgrounds should be indicated on the preliminary plan in order that it may be determined when and in what manner such areas will be dedicated to, or acquired by the appropriate taxing agency. In general, whenever the proposed subdivision contains 20 acres or includes more than 100 lots, consideration shall be given to the reservation or dedication of a suitable area for school and recreation purposes.

In order to insure that sites conformed to the recommendations of the commission in its adopted master plan or portion thereof, the planning commission immediately undertook the development of the requisite master plan. In September, 1955, the commission, in conjunction with the recreation and parks commission and the East Baton Rouge Parish School Board, entered into a contract with a planning consultant for the assembly and analysis of data on existing school facilities and future school population growth.[61] Using the information compiled by the planning consultant, Miss Ruth Wilson, and the planning commission staff, the three agencies worked together to develop the master plan for schools, parks, and playgrounds which was drawn up in final form by the planning commission staff in June, 1956.

On the basis of projected population growth, distribution trends, population density, and trends of school enrollment, the plan suggests a geographical distribution of schools which would meet anticipated needs as of 1970. It should be emphasized that the master plan does not dictate specific sites, but indicates the general areas within which schools will be needed as demographic characteristics of the parish demand them.[62] The accompanying map is that portion of the master school plan for rural (nonsuburban) elementary schools, Figure XII.

With the adoption of the city-parish subdivision ordinance and the master school plan, there was, for the first time since the inception of the new form of government, an effective, workable, and logical procedure for locating schools to take account of present and future educational needs of the rural area of the parish.[63] In fact, although there were provisions in the city subdivision ordinance of 1949 which were similar to those in the 1955 parish-wide ordinance relative to the commission's role in the location of school sites (section VII), it had not been the practice to rely on professional planning for the locations of schools in either the city or parish prior to 1955. The 1949 city subdivision ordinance was somewhat loosely drawn and the provisions for reservation of sites for public purposes were not mandatory. Furthermore, even the discretionary provisions depended on the adoption of a master plan, and this was not accomplished until 1956; in practice part of the city subdivision ordinance was virtually meaningless.[64]

To supplement the orderly procedure for the location of schools provided through the actions described above, the planning commission and the school board came to a policy agreement in 1957 which further allowed the planning commission to influence school site selection. The agreement provided a basis for informal coordination between the two agencies in their mutual efforts to select the "best sites" for schools. It is significant that the school board has defined "best site" as "the site which most closely follows sound planning principles in keeping with the official Master Plan for Schools, which

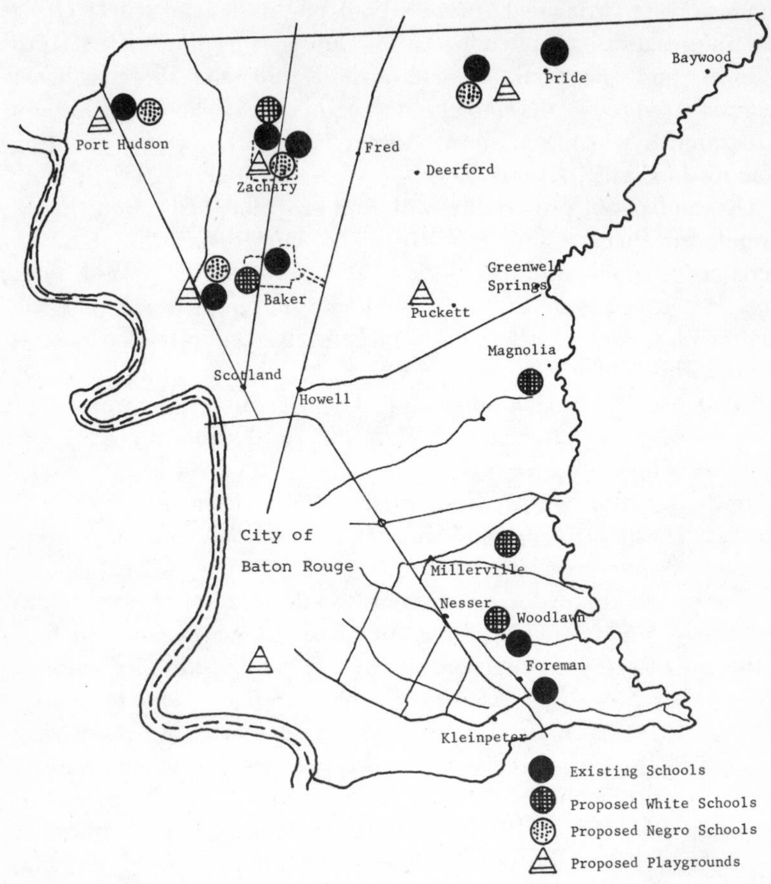

FIGURE XII Planned Locations for Rural Elementary Schools in East Baton Rouge Parish

was adopted on June 25, 1956."[65] Furthermore, the school board suggested that its staff work with the planning commission, through its member on the commission, and the director of planning in attempting to locate such "best sites." Finally, the board, after approving its staff's recommendation, would solicit the final approval of the planning commission before notifying the property owner of its proposed choice of site. Actually, this agreement was an effort to systematize and to put into writing a cooperative pattern which had developed between the commission and the board at least as far back as the joint development of the master plan for schools.[66] The extent of the cooperation which began taking shape in 1955 is indicated by the accompanying résumé (Table 8) of schools built and sites acquired between 1955 and 1960.[67] During this period, the planning commission had the opportunity to influence the location of school sites in three general ways. The most popular mode of influence has been through direct adherence to the master plan. In this case, school sites have been acquired in conformity with the projected school requirements of population dispersal patterns as envisaged by the planning commission, Table 8. Secondly, in areas

TABLE 8
City and Parish Schools Built Between 1935 and 1960, East Baton Rouge Parish

School	City	Parish	How Influenced+
Bakersfield		W*	Master Plan
Baker Heights		W	Informal
Broadmoor High		W	Master Plan
Capital Elementary	C*		Informal
Capital High	C		Master Plan
Glasgow Junior High	W		Master Plan
Glenoaks Junior High		W	Master Plan
Greenbriar Elementary		W	Informal
Jefferson Terrace Elem.		W	Master Plan
Lanier		W	Master Plan
Lee High	W		Informal
Magnolia Woods		W	Master Plan
Mayfair		C	Informal
McKinley High	C		Master Plan
Northdale Elementary	W		Informal
Polk Elementary	C		Master Plan
Progress Elementary		C	Master Plan
Red Oaks Elementary		W	Master Plan
Scotlandville High		C	Master Plan
Sharon Hills		W	Master Plan
South Greenville Elem.	C		Master Plan
University Terrace	W		Master Plan
Villa Del Rey Elem.		W	Subdivision
Westdale Elementary		W	Master Plan
White Hills Elementary		W	Informal
Zachary Elementary		W	Informal
Summary by origin.			
Master Plan	6	11	
Subdivision	-	1	
Informal	3	5	
	9	17	

*C = Colored School
W = White School

+All sites were acquired after the Plan of Government went into operation, except Lee High, acquired in 1944. In addition, the school board acquired three sites, but have not yet constructed schools on them in Westminster, Sherwood Forest, and Marydale Subdivisions. The locations of these schools were influenced by the provisions of the subdivision ordinance pertaining to schools.

where school needs were unforeseen by the master plan, the commission has influenced the selection of school sites by informal means, usually through personal coordination by staff members of the two agencies. Finally, some school sites have been acquired through the method afforded by section VII of the city-parish subdivision ordinance.

Almost twice as many schools were constructed in the rural area of the parish between 1955 and 1960 as in the city, which was almost a complete reversal of the trend in the preceding five-year period. And the planning commission exercised a positive influence in the location of *every school built in the rural area in the period 1955-60.*

A complementary service provided by the planning commission to the school authority arises because the former agency's recommendations on school sites take into consideration the location and anticipated location of major streets and roads. Because it is not desirable, for reasons of safety, to construct elementary schools on major thoroughfares, the commission's advice on trends of traffic flow is beneficial to the school board. Prior to the planning commission's operation, advice of this nature was not readily available; consequently, major rural schools such as Pride, Zachary, Central, and Woodlawn (all of which have children of elementary school age and all of which were located without the benefit of planning commission advice) are immediately adjacent to state highways. One staff member of the school board, who has a primary responsibility for preliminary selection of school sites, suggests that these schools would not be so unwisely located today. The same school administrator summarizes the relationship[68] between the school board and the planning commission as follows:

> The finest thing the City-Parish government has done for us (the School Board) has been to provide assistance in selecting school sites. Today, we wouldn't think of building a school without the advice of the City-Parish Planning Commission.

Capital Improvements Planning

Perhaps in keeping with the desires of its drafters, the plan of government was rather vague concerning the powers to be granted the nascent planning commission. One of its two stated powers and duties was to:[69]

> ... prepare and revise annually a program of capital improvements, for the parish and city respectively, for the ensuing five years, and it shall submit the same annually to the mayor-president at such time as he shall direct, together with estimates of the cost and recommendations as to the means of financing such capital improvements to be undertaken in the ensuing fiscal year and in the next four years, as the basis of the capital budgets to be submitted by the mayor-president to the councils. In the preparation of its capital budget recommendations the planning commission shall consult with the mayor-president, the heads of departments, the school board, state officials, and interested citizens and organizations, and shall hold such hearings as it shall deem necessary.

Since the charter went into effect in 1949, the planning commission has dutifully submitted its proposed capital improvements program to the mayor-president. As has previously been indicated, there were existing and growing needs for large-scale capital improvements in the parish at the time of the charter's adoption. Basically the greatest needs were for a parish-wide drainage system and for the construction of a modern network of streets in the newly incorporated areas of the city. The improvement of rural roads in the parish was not considered a necessity at this time as those areas outside the city limits were still thinly populated and vehicular traffic was light on parish maintained roads. Therefore it was to be expected that the planning commission, in its first proposed budgets, would concentrate on the former areas. Generally this proved to be the case; the planning commission, working largely through special committees, recommended the passage of a large bond issue to carry out an extensive program of street and drainage improvements. However, no proposed bond issue was adopted by the parish council for submission to the voters until 1953, four years after the planning commission's first capital improvements budget was sent to the mayor-president. In view of the widespread recognition among officials of the city-parish needs at this time, why this long delay? The answer is largely related to political problems confronting the new government. The adoption of the charter had been bitterly opposed by a strong and highly vocal group in the city and parish which had come within three hundred votes of securing the rejection of the plan of government. Strong opposition to the new form of government continued after consolidation was carried at the polls. Recognizing the strength and depth of anti-charter feeling, the first mayor-president attempted to pursue a moderate, noncontroversial course. In addition, the mayor-president was handicapped by illness for a considerable time. He did not press for council approval of the capital improvement budgets submitted by the planning commission, apparently feeling that there were grave risks in asking the public to assume a large burden of debt at this time, and a severe defeat of a proposed bond issue might hinder the new government's eventual chances for success. Hence, the 1949-52 administration did little toward implementing the planning commission's proposed capital improvements program.

With the election of Jesse Webb, Jr., to the mayor-presidency in 1952, this cautious approach to a public improvements bond issue referendum was abandoned. During his first year in office, Webb approved and secured council endorsement of the planning commission's proposed capital improvements budget. A five-year capital improvements program, to be financed by a $40.3 million bond issue, was undertaken. Mayor-President Webb, the planning commission, and Colonel J. Lester White, director of the public works department, apparently thought that the parish electorate could be persuaded to adopt this ambitious program, since they spearheaded a major campaign to secure approval. The support of the city's newspapers, the Lions, Rotary, and Kiwanis clubs, the Junior Chamber of Commerce, and most city-parish officials was enlisted. Despite a great promotion effort, the proposed issue was beaten in July, 1953, by a popular vote of more than two to one. To some extent, anti-charter sentiment was undoubtedly a factor in the defeat. The negative vote was very heavy in North Baton Rouge and the northern rural areas of the parish.[70] The public had seemingly not adjusted to the need for capital improvements and was unaccustomed to being confronted with such comprehensive proposals in contrast to the piecemeal practices of the past.

The defeat of the planning commission's initial capital improvements plan resulted in serious reappraisal by the commission and the planning staff. The defeated program had been prepared without any great effort to fathom the opinion of the various segments of the community. If it was professionally determined that a certain project was needed, this was usually sufficient to warrant its inclusion in the commission's program.[71] This independent course was abandoned after the staff and commission read the election returns. Work was begun on a new capital improvements program which would not only meet the urgent needs of the parish, but which could also secure voter approval. The following action was taken:

...in 1953, the Planning Commission requested Civic Clubs, Labor Unions, Parent-Teacher Associations and other groups to send members of their clubs to sit down and talk over plans for the betterment of the streets and drainage of our parish. Each organization sent a representative. These citizens represent a cross-section of the parish. After nearly two years of meetings, they recommended a plan which they had carefully worked out.[72]

The planning commission's capital improvements budget for 1955 was not nearly as ambitious as the 1953 program. The new plan included only drainage and street and road projects whose construction was deemed urgent by the planning commission. Eight drainage projects were to be authorized and over $8,000,000 in street and road projects were outlined. Funds were also set aside to cover engineering costs on future drainage and road surveys. It was strongly emphasized that while the program would cost over $10,000,000, the parish's burden would be only about half this amount. Local costs were to be met by a "pay as you go" five mill tax on property for three years. Of these five mills, 3.88 would be dedicated to streets and roads and 1.12 to the completion of a parish drainage system. Home owners would pay only about one million dollars in taxes for this program as industry, business, and homestead exemption would cover the rest. This smaller, more clearly defined program neutralized the objections of many of the opponents of the 1953 bond issue. The rural sections stood to gain considerably from the program as protection against flood conditions would be greatly increased and nearly a million dollars were to be spent on paving rural roads. On April 5, 1955, the voters approved the five mill program. The long preparation and work by the planning commission and the planning staff had finally borne fruit.

Since the passage of this program the planning commission has had little success with getting its capital improvements budgets adopted. A $21,000,000 bond issue was passed in 1959 to finance trunk sewers, treatment plants, and pumping stations for the consolidated sewer district in East Baton Rouge Parish. Since funds from the three year-five mill tax program voted in 1955 were almost depleted a $41,000,000 bond issue was proposed in 1957, but the voters of the parish rejected this, and it is generally agreed that a renewal of the five mill tax might have been received more favorably. Except for the sewer bond issue, no capital improvements program has been submitted to the people, capital improvements having been met out of recurring revenues. In 1962, however, the mayor-president and the councils aproved the planning commission's recommended five-year "pay as you go" capital improvements budget. In substance, the planning commission and planning staff have continued to follow the formula which led to the successful budget adoption in 1955.

Chapter IV

Public Works and Related Rural Area Services

The Police Jury System and Roads and Drainage in Rural East Baton Rouge Parish

THE MOST IMPORTANT task of the police jury under the pre-1949 system of local government was its direction of the parish department of public works. Some special problems existed in this connection because, while the Fourth, Fifth, Seventh and Tenth Wards were entirely rural in composition, the Third, Sixth, Eighth, and Ninth Wards contained part of the urbanized area of Baton Rouge, in addition to rural sectors. The department of public works, which, of course, was responsible for maintaining the parish roads and drainage system, operated on a budget of $475,000 during the year of 1947.[1] This represented slighty over half of the total parish budget of $915,400.00. During 1947, the police jury approved bids in the amount of $250,571.33 for paving streets and laying sidewalks. All of these projects lay within the metropolitan area of Baton Rouge outside the city limits. Bids on equipment totaling $10,740.28 were approved. These figures convey some idea of the size of the department at this time and of the relative burden that it had to undertake in providing essentially urban services to an area legally classified as rural. The proportionate volume of public works of an urban nature being carried out by a governmental body designed for rural purposes is in itself an indication that the police jury was not merely overseeing certain urban services in an ad hoc manner, but this constituted a major portion of its work. At the same time, the organizational approach was still very much in the tradition of extreme rural decentralization of administrative responsibility and functions. A former member of the parish police jury described that body's system of running the public works department in this way: "It was antiquated. Each member was actually the director of public works for his own ward. Needless to say, a great deal of confusion and bickering occurred on the jury resulting in a lack of coordination in carrying out a public works program."[2]

In an attempt to reduce the quarreling and confusion and to increase coordination, the police jury set up (in 1944) a public works committee to be composed of from five to seven members, who were to direct the public works department subject to the approval of the entire police jury. This committee was retained until the police jury was replaced in 1949. It is questionable whether direction of the department of public works by this committee represented any real concentration either of authority or responsibility. The quarreling and dissension among the jurors was as pronounced within the committee as on the police jury at large. For example, a Baton Rouge newspaper reported that the following incident occurred at the public works committee meeting on September 8, 1947:

> A heated argument arose later in the meeting when Fred Broussard, Sixth Ward, learned that the new dragline is presently doing work in the Tenth Ward. Broussard maintained that the Tenth Ward work had not been authorized by the committee and pointed out that the work on Bayou Duplantier in the Sixth Ward was authorized three years ago.
>
> The matter was not settled until the committee, over Philander Smith's protests, voted to remove the new dragline from the Tenth Ward to the Sixth Ward for the Bayou Duplantier job.[3]

The public works committee scheduled meetings about once a month, but the absence of a quorum sometimes prevented the group from transacting business. The regular meeting on July 21, 1947, failed to produce a quorum and the *Morning Advocate* reported: "One of the persons asked how often the group called meetings and then failed to get a quorum. To this, Smith (a juror) replied, 'The same thing happened one month from this night.' "[4]

Fred Broussard, a member of the public works committee on the police jury, had earlier attacked the system of directing the department in the following statement: " 'Regardless of how honest we may all be," he said after listing the good things that the public works committee had done, 'when we place the public works on a ward basis we naturally fight each other for as much as we can get for our wards.'

" 'The ward system is the way of inefficiency and politics and not the way of the good of the parish,' he said." [5]

Among the criticisms leveled at the department of public works as operated under the police jury was one by W. P. Barnes, a member of the police jury, at a regular meeting of the jury on August 1, 1947, during the heat of the campaign to adopt the new city charter:

> "What the opponents of the charter failed to mention is that the police jury's department of public works now employs a foreman and maintains a road crew in each of the eight wards oustide the city," Barnes charged. "Under the new charter our road system would be districted on a basis of mileage rather than by wards, and a considerable saving effected by greater efficiency."
>
> He attacked the present governmental setup as weak and particularly singled out the department of public works, characterizing it as "big business" since it had a budget of approximately $425,000 for 1947.[6]

These general charges of administrative inadequacies by police jury members tend to be borne out by the actual conditions in the parish with respect to roads, drainage, and planning under the police jury system. Prior to 1949, the parish road system consisted entirely of gravel and dirt roads with the exception of the paved streets which were within the suburban area adjacent to city limits of Baton Rouge. The maintenance of streets and roads was on a ward basis. Each ward had its own road foreman and a road crew of about eight men with the exception of Ward Three, where a larger work force was required. T. N. Samuel, Ward Four road foreman under the police jury and present superintendent of the public works department's rural streets and roads division, commented about conditions under the police jury:

> There was very little equipment and the little that was available was in very poor condition. With the exception of the Third, each ward averaged one truck, one tractor and a pull grader, none of which was anywhere near new.

In my ward we tried to grade the gravel roads about once a month. I believe this was the procedure in the other wards.[7]

A pamphlet published in 1957 summed up the parish road situation as it existed ten years earlier:

As late as ten years ago, few people thought of the parish road system as an important part of the traffic program of the community. Subdivisions and industrial developments in the parish were scattered and we depended on state and federal roads in the parish to carry the small amount of commerce and traffic outside of the city limits. Improvements were based on need at the time and limited by a shortage of funds.[8]

Drainage has long been a pressing problem in East Baton Rouge Parish. Although the parish lies along one of the world's largest rivers, the Mississippi, over 95 per cent of its land area is drained by the Comite-Amite River system. The reason for this is that the spring flood of the Mississippi long ago built a high bank on the river's east side which causes most rainfall in the parish to drain away from the Mississippi rather than toward it. Consequently, East Baton Rouge Parish is drained by a number of small streams, which, in general, flow east and south into the Comite and Amite rivers. As there is only a gentle slope in most parts of the parish, these streams (such as Jones Creek, Claycut Bayou, and Ward's Creek) flow very slowly. In heavy rains the gravity flow of these waterways is inadequate; furthermore, the Comite-Amite River system often cannot handle the water discharged into it, and a "backup" of water into the small streams takes place. These streams then overflow into the adjacent lands at frequent intervals. Land development within the parish has tended to increase the seriousness of the drainage problem. Undeveloped land that lies out as pasture or woods is able to absorb much more of the rainfall than does a developed area with its rooftops, streets, and drainage ditches. By 1947, the rapid development of land in East Baton Rouge Parish had reduced the absorbency to the point at which practically every heavily concentrated rainfall resulted in considerable inundation, extending even to some large residential areas. The police jury never made more than temporary piecemeal efforts to solve this problem. Some drainage work was undertaken over the years, such as the dredging of Ward's Creek and Jones Creek. But these projects did not begin to affect the overall drainage situation. Concerning these projects undertaken by the police jury, the parish engineer made the following point in the discussions preceding the adoption of the parish budget for 1948: "In the discussion of appropriating the $100,000 for drainage, Sam Dupree, parish engineer, pointed out that the drainage problem would have to be tackled as a parish-wide project. Temporary reliefs, he explained, only turned drainage water from one section of the parish to another, not solving the problem."[9] As a specific example of the inadequacy of the parish's drainage system, the events of March 13 and 14, 1947, may be cited. Eight and a half inches of rain fell in a single night on this occasion. Many areas were flooded, many families were marooned, and a number of major roads were blocked.[10]

The flood here focused attention on the need for improvements in the local drainage situation.

Sam G. Dupree, parish engineer, pointed out yesterday morning that the state department of public works and the East Baton Rouge police jury have worked out a parish-wide drainage program which would give the city and parish permanent drainage facilities. These proposals are to be submitted soon to the police jury looking toward calling a bond issue to finance the project.

He said the drainage program would cost about $2,000,000 and could be completed in two years. It would cover dredging of canals in the metropolitan areas, among other things. [By contrast with the need observed, the earlier efforts of the police jury to solve the drainage problem are indicated by the setting aside of a drainage reserve of only $20,000 in the 1947 budget.]

The special drainage fund, committee members pointed out, was set aside when there was hope for launching a state-assisted, parish-wide drainage program. Since the plan has apparently fallen through, they explained, the earmarked funds could be turned back to the general expense account.[11]

The money was turned back to the general expense account and was used to finance a 10 per cent pay raise for public works employees.

A summary of the drainage situation just as the new city-parish government took office included the following comments:

One of the biggest problems facing the new city-parish government, and one that will have to be met, is that of drainage.

In their plan, representatives of Harland Bartholomew and Associates estimated that adequate drainage for the rural and urban areas will cost more than any project still to be tackled in the parish other than an extensive street and highway improvement program.

> Folks living in the rural areas of the parish are well aware also, of the damage done to their land by the lack of drainage facilities.[12]

Even though there was no comprehensive planning and no planning agency under the pre–1949 governments, it might be supposed that engineering surveys or other forms of preparatory work would have been carried out under the auspices of the public works department in so obviously critical an area as general drainage. However, such was apparently not the case: "No comprehensive planning has ever gone into the drainage work done in East Baton Rouge, but there are indications now [i.e., under the city-parish consolidation] that the increasing need will cause machinery to start moving so something can be done about the situation."[13]

In summary, the parish's department of public works was organized on a ward basis and directed by a committee of the police jury and the jury itself prior to 1949. It was almost inevitable under the circumstances that public works would be disintegrated administratively and that interpersonal relations would prevail over attempts to approach parish needs in the field more objectively, even after population growth and conditions of urbanization had forced the police jury, at least to a limited extent, into activities necessitating a more rational approach to public works administration. The parish road system consisted of a number of gravel and dirt roads, none of which could be called a major road. The drainage system was grossly inadequate as frequent floodings indicated. Such improvements as were being made in roads and drainage were of a temporary nature. No coordination of improvements or comprehensive planning was carried out by the police jury. The jury undoubtedly operated under severe handicaps which were not altogether its fault. Very little in the way of public works could be carried out during the war years, and the effects of the war continued long after 1945. The jury was forced to operate on extremely limited finances and no major capital improvement program could even be considered until more funds were available. After August, 1947, the police jury was operating as a lameduck agency and little could be expected of it under these conditions. The police jury was equipped neither by organizational structures nor by inclination to meet the needs for redevelopment of a program of public works over the parish at large.

The Consoldiated Department of Public Works

Under the new city-parish government, a department of public works was developed which differed significantly from its predecessor. Since rural road and street maintenance and drainage were continued as responsibilities of this department, a comparison of organization and procedure with the previous system is in order. The *Plan of Government* provides that "there shall be for East Baton Rouge Parish and the City of Baton Rouge a single unified department of public works the head of which shall be the director of public works." [14]

In brief, the chief executive officer of the city and parish (the mayor-president) has the power to appoint and remove the director of public works. The charter further provides that:

> The director of public works shall be a qualified civil engineer, licensed to practice his profession under the laws of this state, with at least five years practical experience in public works or highway administration. He shall have the general management and control of the several divisions of the department of public works and, subject to the provisions of Chapter 9 [i.e., the Civil Service provision] of this plan of government, shall appoint and remove all the officers and employees of the department and shall have power to make rules and regulations for the conduct of its business consistent with this plan of government and the ordinances of the parish and city councils.[15]

The director is aided in his work by an assistant director who serves immediately under him. The *Plan of Government* expressly provided for only seven functional divisions, but the council was given the power to create others as needed. At the present time there are twelve divisions within the department.

As the city-parish plan of government provides for the financing of some divisions by the city council, some by the parish council, and others on a joint basis, the department has both a city budget and a parish budget. For example, appropriations for street and road maintenance, engineering, and rural bridge, canal, and sewer maintenance are made by the parish council, whereas the city council provides funds for refuse collection, and urban bridge, canal, and sewer maintenance and inspection. Thus, while the department of public works is a "unified department" with a single direction, a certain dualism exists because it must operate on two budgets. A. M. Rosenthal, the present director of public works, made the following comments on this situation: "Of course we can't use city appropriations for parish work or parish funds for city work, but we have been able to shift a work crew from the city to the parish or vice versa for a short length of time if the need was critical. This has served to lessen the effects of the territorial division of the parish into two distinct maintenance areas." [16]

Public works has been and remains the largest department of the city-parish government. As its budgets indicate, it has experienced a rapid growth over the past decade. The annual parish public works appropriation rose from $467,062 in 1944-47 to $1,405,655 in 1958-61, an increase of over 200 per cent. By comparison, the city's annual appropriation for the public works department totaled $233,632 in 1944-47 and $2,152,052 in 1958-61, or an increase of over 800 per cent. The combined budgets gave the department of public works a total annual appropriation of $3,547,707 during the period 1958-61. The department of public works currently employes a work force of about 700 employees. The rural road and street maintenance division has a strength of 58 men while rural bridge, canal, and sewer maintenance has 67 men, 27 of whom are in the rural bridge and canal maintenance section. Within the department, the division of engineering designs and prepares plans, specifications, and estimates for and supervises the construction of all improvements which are undertaken by the city or parish.

In an attempt to secure greater efficiency, the *Plan of Government* provided for the department of public works: "The division of central garage, authority to establish which is hereby granted to the parish council, which shall, when established, store, maintain, and repair cars, trucks and other movable equipment belonging to the parish, the city, or any district of which the parish council or city council is the governing body." [17] Under the police jury, each ward crew was required to keep up its own equipment. Today this added responsibility is spared the maintenance units and they can devote full time to their primary jobs. All supplies, materials, and equipment purchased by the department of public works are bought through a division of purchasing. If a division in the public works department needs something, the division head writes up a requisition for the needed supplies, material, or equipment and files it with the purchasing agent. Before the purchasing agent can approve the requisition, the director of finance must certify that there is an unexpended and unencumbered balance sufficient to cover the purchase in the division's account.

A complaint against one aspect of this system of purchasing was voiced by the superintendent of the rural bridge, canal, and sewer maintenance division in the public works department, and concurred in by the superintendent of the rural road and street maintenance division: "In some ways there was more efficiency in the old system. There are too many complications in getting action today. It's very hard to get any replacement parts. The purchasing system causes a great deal of delay and some means of expediting purchases is needed. If you needed something quickly under the old system you could get it without so much trouble or delay." [18] Each division within the department of public works is required to submit an estimate of its expenditures and material needs for the coming quarters. This estimate is used in determining what the division's quarterly allotment will be. In some public works divisions, such as the central garage, expenditures and material needs for the coming three months can be guaged fairly accurately. However, in the rural road and street maintenance division and the rural bridge, canal, and sewer maintenance division, the quarterly estimate is little more than a guess. These divisions work outdoors and hence are at the mercy of the elements. During a quarter of frequent and heavy rainfall, little work can be done, thus expenditures are low, but if a long period of good weather prevails, much work is undertaken and costs are very high. If this happens, the division must draw on the department's general fund to cover expenditures. However, the yearly budget estimates as submitted by the divisions are surprisingly close to the actual expenditures, as nature's extremes tend to balance out over a year's time.

Somewhat like the city-parish government as a whole, the department of public works is a "compound-functional consolidation" rather than a completely unified department. The department is administratively consolidated in terms of overall direction and supervision, central garage functions, personnel administration, major works planning and coordination, and purchasing. But in budgetary allocations and actual units, there is still a clear separation between rural and urban administration. The latter condition recognizes the two local government organizations — city and parish — as opposed to complete unity. To some extent, however, the internal departmental differences merely represent the normal organization or administration along functional lines that occur *within any governmental department;* and the unified direction of the agency apparently permits considerable flexibility in temporarily transferring work crews to areas of immediate need, regardless of the strict lines between parish and city.

In comparison with the previous system of amateur supervision of the public works function by part-time elective officials who operated within a framework of complete administrative disintegration, the present department is administratively and politically responsible as a unit, is organized and staffed in terms of professional standards, is able to plan and execute public works programs for the entire geographic area of the parish, and carries out its auxilliary functions – e.g., purchasing and equipment maintenance – centrally. The acid test of organization improvement, however, is the extent to which the change increases the level and volume of service.

The Parish Road System under the City-Parish Government

As has just been pointed out, when the new government took over in 1949, it inherited a rudimentary system of gravel and dirt roads and little else. The existing equipment was in poor condition and a ward basis of maintenance was established practice, with a foreman and a crew in each ward. The road maintenance system was almost completely reconstructed under the new city-parish government. Within the department of public works a rural streets and roads division was established to maintain the parish road system. Four maintenance districts were established, each with approximately the same amount of mileage to keep up. For the first three years or so, the parish department of public works operated on a budget of around a half-million dollars, and its rural streets and roads division received about one-fourth of this amount. In 1952, the division's budget was $132,000; in 1953, $162,000. By 1955, the parish public works department's budget was increasing rapidly and the rural streets and roads maintenance budget reached $195,000. A steady yearly increase was maintained with the division being allocated $288,000 in 1958, and $344,000 in 1961. In 1962 (a year of austerity for the city), for the first time since 1950, a reduction was made in the division's budget to $315,000 for the year. In this most recent budget year, approximately one-fifth of the total parish public works' budget was allocated to this division.

The fiscal pattern for this division is incomplete without some reference to the capital improvements made in the road system under the city-parish government. In 1951, the first major rural road capital improvement projects were launched by the parish. With the state furnishing the sand, clay, and gravel, the city-parish providing the black-top, and the public works department doing the work on three major projects, some ten miles of road was black-topped at a total cost of over $124,000. In connection with these state aid projects, the 1951 city-parish annual report stated: "Parish roads are selected for state aid on the basis of use, the state department of highways making frequent traffic counts. Other parish roads are maintained by the department of public works with the state furnishing $30,000 of gravel annually." [19] During the following years, few capital improvements were undertaken as the city-parish voters rejected the $40.3 million bond issue in 1953. Finally, with the approval of the five mill tax improvements program in 1955, several new rural road projects were initiated.

Another large bond issue, which would have financed the construction of a system of improved parish roads, failed in 1957. Despite this setback, the city-parish government continued to finance a capital improvements program out of recurring sources of revenue. Excess revenue bonds and special appropriations were used as the methods of financing. One and a half million dollars in excess revenue bonds were sold by the city in 1959 to finance rural road improvements. The parish budget for 1959 provided $200,000 for blacktopping and improving rural roads and streets. In 1961, the parish council provided $50,000 dollars for similar purposes. As 1962 was a "tight" year for the city financially, no new rural road capital improvement projects were authorized and none are under construction at this time. The specific projects carried out under these allocations are shown on the accompanying map, Figure XIII.

A summary of the major parish road improvement projects reveals their cost to the city-parish government at over two million dollars. This sum, while not tremendous, is significant when one remembers that with the exception of the three-year five mill tax program, the voters of East Baton Rouge Parish have consistently defeated capital improvement bond issues. As a result of these projects, the Parish of East Baton Rouge now boasts over sixty miles of rural blacktop roads, whereas in 1949 not a single mile of non-

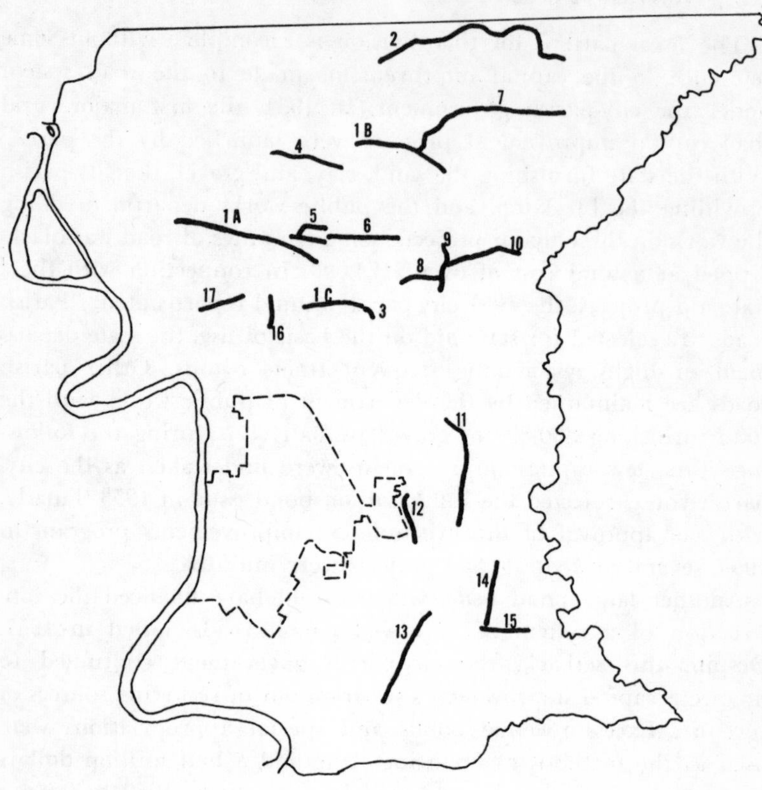

Number	Name	Length	Cost*	Source of Funds	Time
1-A	Groom Road	5.0			
1-B	Deerford Rd	3.5	$125,000	Special Appropriation	1951
1-C	Comite Drive	2.0			
2	Pride-Port Hudson Rd	6.6	151,000	Excess Revenue Bonds, 1959	1959-60
3	Comite Drive	1.1	42,000	5-mill tax funds	1958
4	Lower Zachary Road	2.9	126,000	Excess Revenue Bonds, 1959	1959
5	Rolling Acres-Bentley Drive	2.5	88,000	Special Appropriation	1959
6	Dyer Road	3.1	143,000	Excess Rev. Bonds, '59	1959-60
7	Milldale Rd.	7.2	320,000	5-mill tax funds	1957-59
8	Core Lane	1.5	81,000	Special Appropriation	1959-60
9	Joor Road	2.0	60,000	5-mill tax funds	1956-57
10	Denham Road	3.2	155,000	Excess Rev. Bonds. '59	1959-60
11	Flannery Rd.	5.3	269,000	Special Appropriation	1958-61
12	Sharp Road	1.6	76,000	Special Appropriation	1961-62
13	Siegen Lane	4.0	210,000	Special Appropriation	1959-61
14	Germany Road	2.7	75,000	Special Appropriation	1959-60
15	Tiger Bend Rd.	1.3	70,000	Special Appropriation	1958-59
16	Gibbens Road	.8	45,000	Special Appropriation	1959-60
17	Thomas Road	1.6	50,000	Special Appropriation	1961
Totals		57.9	$2,086,000		1951-63

*Cost figures rounded to nearest thousand.

FIGURE XIII Major City-Parish Road Projects Completed, 1951-62

urban blacktop existed. In addition to its improved roads, the parish maintains about three hundred and forty miles of gravel roads and some ten miles of dirt roads.[20] (See Figure XIV.) Today, the third maintenance district at Central, which has fourteen men, does nothing but maintain the parish's asphalt roads. The first district at Baker with twenty men, the second at Pride with ten, and the fourth at Woodlawn with twelve, work the gravel roads in their areas and assist the asphalt unit in keeping up the blacktopped roads in their districts.

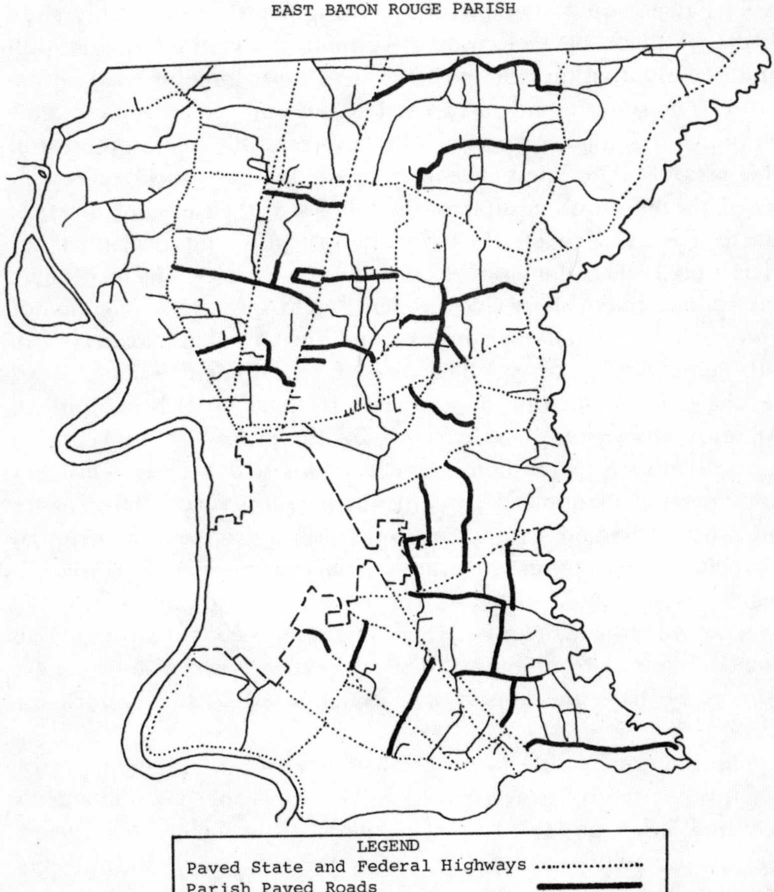

FIGURE XIV Road System, East Baton Rouge Parish, 1962

To furnish a better idea of the extent of activities of the division, the summary of rural streets and road maintenance in the 1959 Annual Report is pertinent. In addition to maintaining over 350 miles of gravel and dirt roads, this division completely rebuilt 2.07 miles of asphalt roads by applying three shots (layers) of asphalt and repaired 17.1 miles of blacktop by putting a seal coat down with one shot of asphalt. On Essen Lane 2.1 miles were repaired by digging out the soft spots and concreting them and then patching the road with two shots of asphalt. Two dead-end roads, Packard and Steam, were opened into school property.[21]

The road equipment picture has brightened considerably since 1949. In place of each ward's wornout truck, tractor, and pull grader, this division now possesses a modern force of road equipment. The superintendent of rural streets and roads reports: "Our equipment is good, very good. We have certainly made progress in this area." [22] The latest inventory in the public works department listed the division's equipment as follows: eight cars and pickups; thirteen trucks, ten of which are dump trucks; one personnel carrier; one 1,500-gallon asphalt distributor; thirteen tractors; three caterpillar tractors; twelve graders, eight of which are motor graders; one gradall; five rollers; and two front-end loaders with two cubic yard buckets.[23] The division's equipment is maintained by the city-parish's central garage as is all city-parish equipment. At the present time, the division is in the process of replacing all its pull graders with motor graders. This will increase efficiency and conserve manpower. In general, the rural roads maintenance units have adequate equipment to perform the many tasks required of them. An exception is the asphalt maintenance section. According to its foreman, "this unit must have more dump trucks. We weren't able to get them last year because of the city-parish government's financial troubles, but our prospects are very good for next year as we have the approval of everyone up to the Council for them." [24]

The division is able to do a fairly good job of keeping up the extensive system of gravel roads. In this area only maintenance is required as no gravel roads of significance are being constructed. In fact, the number of miles of parish gravel roads has been declining for some ten years or so as more and more blacktopping takes place. Under the police jury gravel roads were graded about once a month, but the roads superintendent now reports: "The gravel roads are graded every week or two weeks, depending on how much they are used." As under the police jury, the state furnishes much of the gravel used to maintain "farm to market" roads, thus relieving the parish of this added expense. Other than this, the state now furnishes no aid toward construction or maintenance of parish asphalt roads. Although the department of public works occasionally constructed a major road in the past, at the present time all important projects are let to contractors for the actual construction. Once a project is accepted as complete by the parish, the asphalt unit must maintain the road. With only fourteen men assigned to this unit, they are often hardpressed to do this.

Many of this division's problems stem from the fact that although it is a rural road and street maintenance unit, it must maintain many miles of streets in near urban and suburban areas. When the city-parish government came into being, Ward One included virtually all of the urban and suburban areas of Baton Rouge. The 1950 census showed that some 124,000 of the parish's 155,000 people lived in the City of Baton Rouge. The population of 30,000 in Wards Two and Three in 1950 had grown to nearly 75,000 by 1960. There are at present some 227 major subdivisions in the area maintained by the rural streets and roads division. The streets in these subdivisions are built by the subdividers but the parish must maintain them, thus constantly increasing the burden of the rural division. As the population in the maintenance area has grown, the demands for the division's services have also greatly increased. A corresponding increase in maintenance manpower has not occurred. The superintendant explained this: "Under the Police Jury we could employ all the laborers we needed for from two to four dollars a day; now a laborer starts at over eleven dollars a day." [25] The 1958 Annual Report of the Department of Public Works stated:

> With its very extensive and broad scope of operation this division spends a great deal of its time going from job to job with its limited personnel and material allotments. It is unfortunate, but the rate of deterioration of our parish roads and streets appears to be accelerating, and although this division unit's efficiency has been improving and will continue to improve with additional equipment, the division is not operating nearly abreast with the requirements for maintenance of these traffic facilities.[26]

The situation described in that report has not yet been much improved. The shortage of manpower is, if anything, more acute. Tasks such as right-of-way clearing, which require considerable hand labor, are far behind schedule. To this date, the city-parish government, not content to depend on the state and federal governments for improved roads, has constructed an important system of blacktopped roads in the parish at a cost of over two million dollars. The maintenance of the gravel and dirt road systems has been continued at an adequate level. In addition, the rural roads division has built up a valuable and modern equipment force since 1949. However, with the rapid increase in population and the corresponding increase in demand for services in its maintenance area, the rural streets and roads division has found itself seriously undermanned in its effort to maintain an adequate parish road system.

Rural Drainage

Much work has been required of the city-parish government in the field of drainage since that program of the city and parish was totally inadequate before the new government was established. The department of public works has separate divisions for city drainage and rural drainage. The rural bridge and canal maintenance division is responsible for all drainage facilities in Wards Two and Three. This unit has experienced a rapid increase in appropriations in the past few years, as have most other divisions in the city-parish public works department. In 1952, $62,000 was allocated for the division (about 12 per cent of the parish's public works appropriations). A budget of $112,000 was approved for the division in 1955. This amount represented nearly 19 per cent of the parish's allotment to the department of public works. During this time the city-parish was rapidly expanding its drainage program. A further increase of $175,000 had occurred by 1959, but by this date the increased amount represented slightly over 13 per cent of the public works expenditures in the parish. Since 1959, the rural bridge and canal maintenance division's budget has remained at about the same level. The 1962 appropriation was only $166,000, which was less than 11 per cent of the parish public works' monies.

Since 1949, a number of capital drainage improvements have been carried out by the city-parish government. One of the first of these was the Ward's Creek project which was financed by the city government, although most of the improvements were in Ward Three. Some $503,000 were appropriated over a three-year period to widen and deepen the small existing channel of Ward's Creek. The three-year, five mill tax program furnished the funds to carry out several major improvement projects. White's Bayou in the northwestern area of the parish was dredged out for a distance of over fourteen miles at a cost of some $283,000. The state contributed 40 per cent of the cost of actual construction, but the city-parish had to secure all rights-of-way and build the needed bridges. The north fork of Ward's Creek was dredged for some four and a half miles at a cost of $75,000 with five mill tax funds. A third major project under this program was the widening and deepening of Jones Creek. The limits of this project reached from the Amite River to the Illinois Central Railroad. Including tributaries of Jones Creek, nearly twenty miles of waterways were improved at a cost of $603,000 to the city-parish government. The state provided 40 per cent of the construction costs. Funds for dredging the lower channel of the Comite River were provided by the five mill special assessment. The state paid 70 per cent of the construction costs for this project. Some $50,000 was appropriated in the 1958 city budget to dredge out Dawson Creek. The completion of this project relieved flooding conditions in part of south Baton Rouge. The final major drainage project approved was the dredging of Claycut Bayou. The 1960 parish budget set aside $290,000 for this purpose.

In addition to these capital improvement projects, the rural bridge and canal maintenance division has done work on a number of jobs with its own men and materials. No contracts are let for drainage projects within the parish unless state funds are involved.[27] The dredging of Bayou Fountain, for example, was done by the maintenance division over a period of four years. It is difficult to estimate the cost of such projects. No satisfactory solution to the drainage problem in East Baton Rouge Parish could have been reached until the Comite-Amite River System was dredged. This action was necessary to prevent water from backing up the parish waterways and flooding the eastern half of the parish. Although the city-parish furnished only a small portion of the funds for work on the Comite River and none for the Amite, its active drainage program within the parish was an important factor in securing federal aid for this project. After years of work by city-parish officials and several members of Louisiana's congressional delegation, a federal appropriation of $4,770,000 was obtained for work on the Comite-Amite System.[28] These funds are being used to finance the dredging of the Amite River from Lake Maurepas to the mouth of the Comite River. A diversion canal connecting the Amite River with Blind River has already been completed.

This brief review of the drainage program carried out in the parish indicates that much has been accomplished under the city parish government. The city-parish councils have appropriated over $2,000,000 for seven major drainage improvement projects. Beyond this, substantial work has been done by the parish's maintenance unit toward constructing an adequate drainage system, and the federal government has made funds available for carrying out an important part of the parish's drainage program. The drainage problem has not yet been completely solved in the parish, but a good start has been made toward that objective. One should bear in mind that the citizens of East Baton Rouge Parish have consistently rejected, with one exception, capital improvement bond issues. Thus, in view of this financial limitation, the accomplishments of the city-parish government in the field of drainage are quite impressive, Figure XV. The securing of funds for, and the

Number	Name	Length	Improvement	Cost	Source of Funds	Time
1	White's Bayou	14.2	Dredged	$ 283,000	5 mill tax funds	1956-58
2	Comite River	10.3	Dredged	286,000	5 mill tax funds	1957-60
3	Jones' Creek	19.7	Widened, deepened & dredged	603,000	5 mill tax funds	1956-58
4	Claycut Bayou*	11.6	Dredged	290,000+	Special Appropriation	1960
5	Ward's Creek, N. Fork	4.5	Dredged	.76,000	5 mill tax funds	1957-58
6	Ward's Creek	7.6	Widened, deepened	503,000#	Special Appropriation	1954-56
7	Dawson Creek	8.8	Widened, deepened	50,000"	Special Appropriation	1958
8	Bayou Fountain	6.0	Enlarge channel	D.P.W. detail	D.P.W. funds	1953-56
Totals		82.7 miles		$2,091,000		

*Under construction.
+Appropriated in 1960 parish budget.
#Appropriated in 1954, 1955, 1956 city budgets.
"Appropriated in 1958 city budget.

Code Explanation for Figure XV

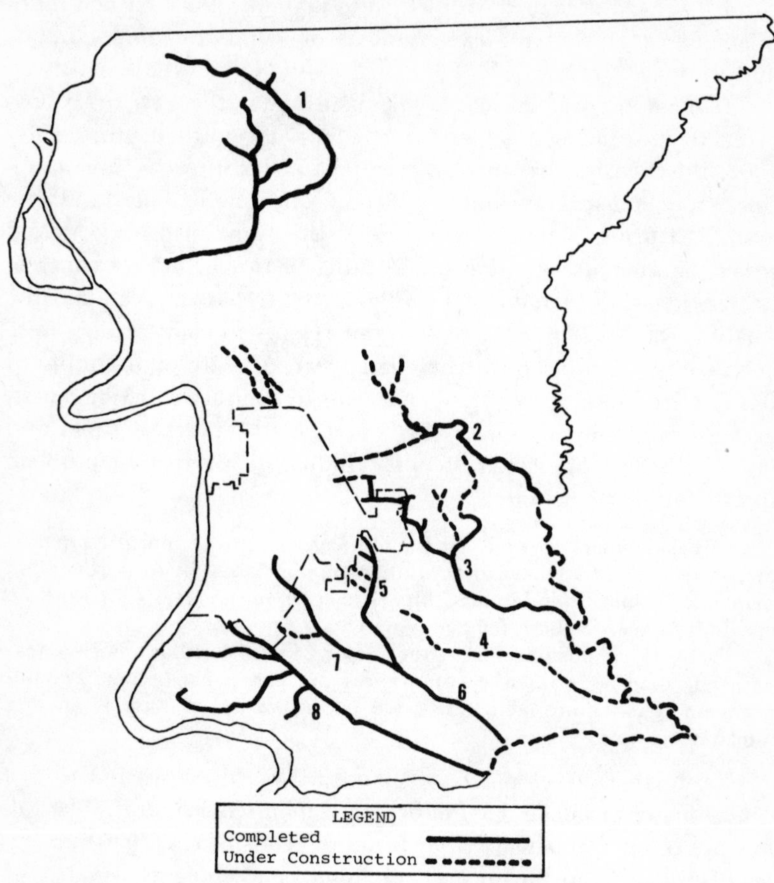

FIGURE XV Drainage System of East Baton Rouge Parish, 1962

construction of major drainage facilities does not, in itself, solve the problem of flooding. The subtropical climate of Louisiana with its heavy rainfall results in a rapid deterioration of canals and drainage ditches. Erosion resulting in frequent cave-ins and the growth of vegetation, such as willows in the canal beds, are the most serious problems facing drainage maintenance units. The job of preventing such recurring developments falls to the rural bridge and canal maintenance division of the public works department. The superintendent of this division has a work force of twenty-seven men in bridge and canal maintenance and forty in rural sewer maintenance with which to maintain the sixty-odd miles of major canals and the two hundred or so miles of minor canals and drainage ditches.

Tremendous progress has been made under the city-parish government in securing good equipment for work on their projects. By 1962, this division had five cars or pick-ups, six trucks, four draglines, four tractors or bulldozers, one personnel carrier, and one gradall. During a typical year, 1958, the rural bridge canal and sewer maintenance division dug 6 miles of canals, built 4 concrete deck bridges, the largest of which was 100 feet by 24 feet, and the smallest was 40 feet by 24 feet. Major repairs to eight bridges were carried out, 75 miles of ditches were cleaned, more than 2 miles of fences were put up, the willows were cut in 10 miles of major canals, and the division cleaned or dug out along 45 miles of street and lateral ditches. The superintendent indicated his greatest problem in the following manner:

> The development and request for drainage has grown much faster than men hired. Today, I have thirty-three common laborers; to do the work demanded, I need one hundred fifty. I have enough requests for work on my desk to keep us busy for five years.
>
> It is nearly impossible to cut the major canals of willows once a year with our shortage of men. Erosion along our canals has become a major problem. The failure to secure wide enough right of ways is another difficulty we face.

The further development of land in Wards Two and Three causes many problems for the drainage maintenance unit. The following often happens: Land formerly classified as pasture frequently flooded in the spring and this was accepted as a matter of course or considered a natural event, whereas today, by contrast, a house goes up in the former pasture and the demand is made for drainage facilities to carry the water off the now suburban yard. Much of the money used in building the parish drainage system came from the federal or state governments, yet when a project was completed, its maintenance became the responsibility of the parish. An already overburdened maintenance unit can scarcely meet this additional demand on its resources. A great deal has been done toward solving the parish's drainage problem but much more remains to be done. While the capital improvements program has moved along at a tolerable pace, the head of drainage maintenance for the parish warns: "Unless more labor is made available, there will be a rapid deterioration of the parish drainage system by the destruction of canals by bushes growing in them, and the erosion of banks. Additional funds for maintenance are sorely needed."[29] Piled-up needs and the necessities created by changing patterns of land use have caused drainage improvement and maintenance of drainage facilities to lag behind current needs. Even so, the recurrent inundations that frequently occurred in almost all the low-lying areas of the parish (including several parts of the city) have largely been brought under control since 1949, by the unified development and extension of the natural drainage system, and the systematic maintenance of these facilities.

Sewerage in East Baton Rouge Parish

The sewerage collection system in Baton Rouge had been largely constructed in the 1930's. Special districts were formed to meet the need for sewerage collection and disposal and bond issues were voted in the new districts to finance the construction of collection systems. Following this, a property assessment would be levied to provide operating funds in each new district. The governing body for these special districts was the parish's governing body, the police jury. After World War II, a substantial portion of the jury's time was devoted to consideration of the sewerage problems of the city and surrounding suburbs. When the new charter was drawn up, the following section provided that these special districts be retained:

> ... sewerage and drainage districts established within East Baton Rouge Parish prior to the first day of January, 1949, whether within or without the City of Baton Rouge, shall continue to exist as on that date constituted to effectuate the purpose for which each was created, to complete any works begun or authorized therein, to pay the debts of the district, and to levy such taxes and other charges as may have been or may be legally authorized in each such district. There shall also be within East Baton Rouge Parish such districts as may be established by the governing body of the parish or city in accordance with the constitution and the general laws of the state.[30]

For several years after the city-parish government was established, the sewerage problems continued to be met by this special district system. Not surprisingly, a sewerage system which had been inadequate in 1949 grew worse. With each district "looking out for itself," the result was chaotic. Districts often had adequate collection lines within their own areas, but lines of adjoining districts often were too small for effective tie-ins. Most sewerage lines emptied into drainage ditches causing a more rapid growth of vegetation and encouraging an increase in mosquitoes, flies, and other parasites. The existing trunk lines were fast becoming obsolete due to the parish's rapid increase in population. Up to this time there had been little, if any, comprehensive planning for an area sanitary sewerage system. It remained for the planning commission to recognize the need for extending the sanitary sewerage facilities throughout the city and into the rapidly growing suburban areas of the parish.

In 1956 a Sanitary Sewage Committee was appointed by the Commission and the Council appropriated funds to prepare a Master Plan.... In February, 1957, the Committee recommended that the engineering consultant firm of Parsons, Brinkerhoff, Hall and MacDonald be engaged to prepare the Master Plan. The Commission entered into a contract with this firm and applied for another planning assistance grant. The Housing and Home Finance Agency subsequently granted $36,500 for half of the estimated cost of the Master Plan. The Consultants presented their first report in November — a preliminary layout of the necessary trunks, mains, pumping stations and treatment plants to serve the City, the Suburban Area and the Towns of Baker and Zachary. A second report on financing methods was presented early in 1958 and the Master Plan was presented in June. After adoption of the Master Plan by the Commission on August 4, 1958, it was recommended to the Council who will take steps toward actual building of the sewer system.[31]

The city-parish council adopted this master plan for sewerage in early 1959 and called an election for May 9, 1959, to establish a consolidated sewerage district and to issue bonds totaling $21 million to construct a system of trunk lines and treatment plants. The proposed district includes about one-fourth of the land area of the parish and some 85 per cent of its population, Figure XVI. The consolidated district includes the industrial area and hence some ten million dollars of the cost is to be borne by industry. Looking to the future, the plan provides ample sewerage facilities to permit normal future development of the area included in the district. For example, in a section zoned for single family dwelling units, the system is designed to care adequately for a family on every available lot, assuming that all usable property is subdivided. The present director of public works estimates that the new sewerage facilities could provide sufficient service for 300,000 people. It

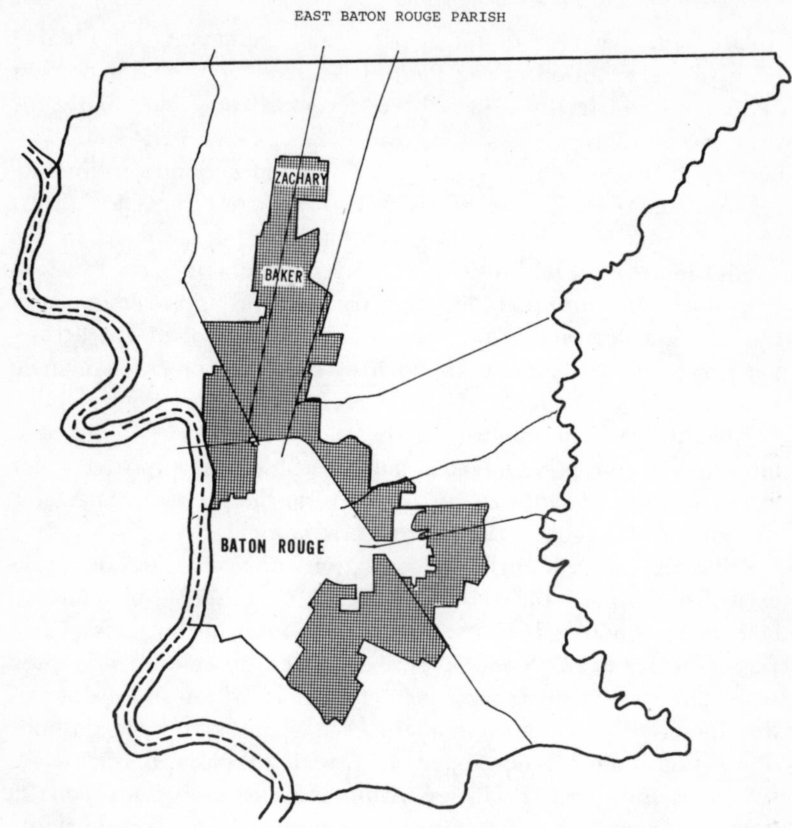

FIGURE XVI Shaded Portion Shows Consolidated Sewer District Area Beyond Baton Rouge City Limits, April, 1959

should be emphasized that the new consolidated district would not interfere with the operation of the older and smaller sewerage districts. The responsibility for the construction of tie-ins and lateral collection lines remained with the local special districts. The sewerage proposals were submitted to the property owners within the proposed district on May 19, 1959. For passage, a majority of both the popular vote and the assessed valuation was needed. In any case, the voters approved the consolidated district and the bond issue necessary to finance it. At the present time the work on the trunk lines and treatment plants is nearing completion.

Recreation and Park Commission

Although the recreation and park commission was consolidated prior to the adoption of the *Plan of Government,* a major portion of its land and facilities have been developed since the plan came into effect. The commission, of course, has its own basic sources of revenue in the form of a one mill ad valorem tax and certain concessions and fees, but it has also had some much-needed direct support from the city-parish government and has shared in the capital improvements program. The recreation and parks function has undergone an unprecedented expansion and improvement since the parish-wide commission was formed. A perusal of the accompanying map will show that much of the development has taken place in the area outside the City of Baton Rouge, Figure XVII. Beyond the evidence shown on the map is the fact that the commission and the school board have continuously improved their relationship in the interest of coordinating the functions and facilities of the two agencies in the recreational field.

Prior to the commission's formation, only two public parks existed in the area: the old City Park (151 acres including a 50-acre lake and a 9-hole golf course), and a small downtown park of two acres (Victory Park). Some other areas were available for organized recreation, but facilities were far below standard for an area of this size. Today, the commission maintains 26 parks and playgrounds comprising some 885 developed acres, with an additional 500 acres yet to be improved. Facilities within these parks include two 18-hole golf courses, two other 9-hole golf courses and an additional 9-hole course that will be 18 holes when completed, a total of 63 buildings, and 119 activity areas. Almost every residential area in the parish now has reasonable access to playgrounds, swimming pools, and related public recreational installations.

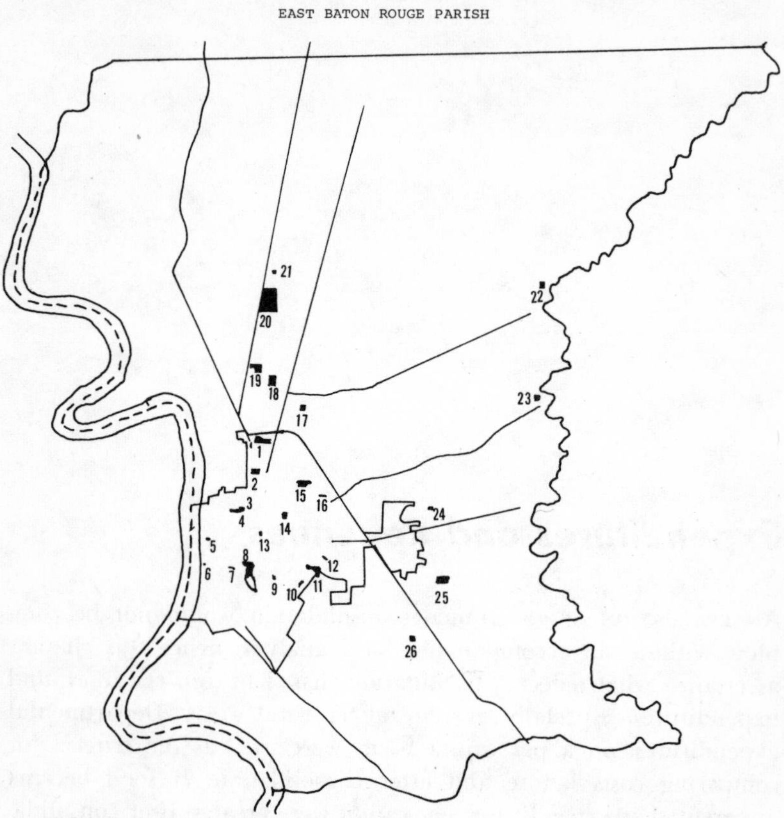

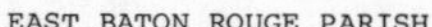

Figure XVII Recreation and Park Facilities in the City and Rural Areas of East Baton Rouge Parish. (1) Monte Sano Park, 40 acres; (2) Kerr-Warren Park, 5.5 acres; (3) Goldsby Field, 9.46 acres; (4) Memorial Stadium, 27.27 acres; (5) Victory Park, 2 acres; (6) Terrace Ave. Recreation Center, 1 acre; (7) Brooks Park, 6.9 acres; (8) City Park, 151 acres including a 50-acre lake; (9) Edward Ave. Park, 0.2 acre; (10) Valley Park, 10 acres; (11) Webb Park, 96.1 acres; (12) Goodwood Playground, 3.5 acres; (13) Progress Playground, 3.5 acres; (14) Capital Ave. Park (Eden Park), 3.46 acres; (15) Howell Park, 114.5 acres; (16) Byrd Station (Lobrano), 4 acres; (17) Fortune Addition, 10 acres; (18) Ryan Field, 40 acres; (19) Jordan Park, 37.45 acres; (20) Greenwood Park, 538 acres and Clark Park, 125 acres; (21) Baker Playground, 10 acres; (22) Jackson Park, 9.55 acres; (23) Greenwell Springs Park, 14.4 acres; (24) Red Oaks Park, 2.08 acres; (25) Forest Park, 115.3 acres; (26) Inniswold Park, 11.13 acres. Victory Park and City Park existed prior to the formation of the recreation and park commission.

Chapter V

Expenditures and Revenues

AN EVALUATION of government consolidation would not be complete without an accompanying fiscal analysis, hence this chapter ascertains what effect consolidation has had on revenues and expenditures, especially as they affect rural areas. Departmental expenditures, on a per capita basis, were used as the criteria for comparing costs before and after consolidation. It soon became apparent that expenditures per capita were greater after consolidation than they were before, even with an adjustment made to correct for the reduced purchasing power of the dollar. Thus, the casual reader may mistakenly conclude that consolidation leads to higher costs. The higher costs, however, cannot be attributed to the consolidation but rather to the dynamic growth which was characteristic of the local economy during the observed period.

Public services expanded at an amazing rate during the early 1950's. The increase in capital expenditures paved the way for many new local developments. New service programs were instituted and public employment increased dramatically. Along with the increased number of employees there came the added cost of new employee benefits. Nevertheless, the increase in expenditures would probably have been more pronounced without consolidation and the benefits derived from coordination of local government services would have been lost. Sources of revenue remained essentially the same as before consolidation but the proportion of funds derived from the various sources showed considerable change because the newly introduced sales tax contributed substantially to total revenues both in the city and in the parish.

TABLE 9

Average Annual Expenditures by Type of Service for the City of Baton Rouge and East Baton Rouge Parish, 1944-47 and 1958-61

Type of Service	Annual Averages*		
	1944-47	1958-61	Per cent 1958-61 is of 1944-47
	(Thousand dollars)		
Legislative and Executive	16	62	388
City	10	15	150
Parish	6	47	783
Judicial	27	104	385
City	10	55	550
Parish	18	50	278
Administration	60	430	717
City	35	190	543
Parish	24	240	1,000
Employee Benefits	--	382	--
City	--	234	--
Parish	--	147	--
Fire Protection	226	1,588	703
City	156	1,588	1,018
Parish	70	--	-100
Police Protection	121	1,603	1,324
City	121	1,603	1,324
Parish	--	--	--
General Services	78	663	850
City	17	486	2,859
Parish	61	177	290
Dept. Public Works	701	3,548	506
City	234	2,142	915
Parish	467	1,406	301
Capital Expenditures	705	1,407	200
City	461	770	167
Parish	244	637	261
Contributions to Constitutional Offices	142	770	542
City	1	150	15,000
Parish	141	621	440
Contributions to Other Agencies	81	98	121
City	56	57	102
Parish	24	40+	167
TOTAL	2,157	10,656	494
City	1,101	7,291	662
Parish	1,057	3,366	318

*Figures rounded to nearest thousand.

+Excludes transfer of 3 mill industrial tax of $534,000 to the municipalities of Baker, Zachary, and Baton Rouge.

Services and Costs

The public services available to residents of East Baton Rouge Parish may be classified into the eleven categories shown in Table 9. These are broad classifications which generally characterize local public services throughout the nation and serve as topical identification for auditing purposes. (Note that these do not include the local school system.) In any auditing procedure, however, one must recognize that the classification of expenditures is not always as precise as would be desirable. Some expenditures could fit equally well under several classifications, and thus the final resting place becomes somewhat arbitrary, particularly with regard to administrative, legislative, executive, and general services. The respective expenditures by each classification may therefore vary slightly, depending upon the grouping of expense items by the auditors or by any statistical analyst. In any case, the totals would not be affected, as this concerns only the allocation of miscellaneous costs by type of service or agency. Tables 23 and 24 (pp. 159-60) indicate more precisely what items of expenditure have been included under the various public service categories. Furthermore, cost comparisons between time periods become clouded because the purchasing power of the dollar changed considerably between the study periods. This is acknowledged by converting 1958-61 costs to 1944-47 dollars. In 1958-61 the dollar had only 65 per cent as much purchasing power as in 1944-47. Even with comparisons made in constant dollars, total parish costs in 1958-61 exceeded costs of 1944-47 in practically every category of expenditures, Table 25.

Legislative and executive costs prior to consolidation include expenditures for the commissioners' and mayor's offices in the city, and the services of the police jury in the parish. After consolidation, this category of expenditures reflected the cost of the city-parish councils and the mayor-president. Total costs, city and parish combined, increased from about $16 thousand per year for the period 1944-47 to about $62 thousand per year for 1958-61, Table 9. Most of the increase in cost was apparent in the parish budget in which legislative and executive costs increased more than seven times. Annual cost to the city was slightly more than $15 thousand in 1958-61 compared to about $10 thousand in 1944-47. Annual per capita cost for this service was 14 cents in 1944-47 and increased to 28 cents in 1958-61; but in terms of constant dollars, there was only a 4 cent per capita increase. The increase in legislative and executive costs following consolidation can be attributed to the expanded activities which necessitated a larger full-time staff, along with higher salaries and related fringe benefits.

Judicial costs, as reported in the city and parish audits, are not a complete accounting of judiciary costs for the parish. A large part of the judicial branch of government is supported by the state through offices established by the state constitution: district court, district attorney, family court, clerk of court, and justices of the peace. Nevertheless, the costs of city court, city clerk, the law library, parish attorney, and juvenile court were met by expenditures from both the city and parish budgets. Judiciary services for city and parish combined increased from about $27 thousand per year in 1944-47 to about $104 thousand per year in 1958-61. City-parish costs, per capita, for this service increased from 24 cents in 1944-47 to 31 cents, in comparable dollars, for 1958-61. In 1944-47, the judicial system in the parish required about $8 thousand more local financial support than the city, but by 1958-61 the city costs exceeded parish costs by $5 thousand. The higher judicial costs may be explained by the enormous increase in volume of legal work, arrests, hearings, and court trials. Much of the earlier service was done on a fee basis, but the increased volume of judicial work demanded larger staffs employed at higher salaries and at greater aggregate costs.

Administration refers to those government services related to the coordination and support of several governmental departments or agencies. These include the department of finance, treasurer, purchasing division, parish clerk, and the personnel department. Furthermore, when travel expenses were not identified as to department, they were counted as part of administration costs. Postage, printing, advertising, auditing, bank charges, and election expenses were also counted under this heading. In 1944-47, the combined total was about $60 thousand per year. By 1958-61, the amount had increased to about $430 thousand per year.

The reorganization of the administrative branch, incident to consolidation, resulted in a greatly expanded work force to cope with the considerable increase in administrative activities. The increased tempo of activity is reflected by the increase in number of pages of minutes which record the official actions taken by the city-parish council after consolidation and by the city commissioners and the police jury before consolidation. The official minutes printed for the city and parish in 1944-47 numbered 1,947 pages; in 1958-61 the minutes numbered 5,387 pages. One can estimate that about three times more business was transacted at this later date. Concomitant to this increased business there would necessarily be a build-up of related activities requiring an appreciable increase in written correspondence, postage, reports, telephones, travel, and processing of payrolls and personnel records. Introduction and administration of the civil service system, operation of the central purchasing division, and the processing of applications for occupational licenses were new services provided by the administrative division. Employee benefits is listed as a subheading under administration. This consists mainly of the matching funds provided by local government for employee insurance, retirement, social security, and other fringe benefits, and which account for a substantial share of the higher administration costs following consolidation. In 1944-47, employee benefits were not distinguished in audited reports for the city and parish, but by 1958-61 the combined total (city and parish) amounted to about $382 thousand per year, Table 9. On a per capita basis the cost of employee benefits was $1.71 per year.

Fire protection services are generally confined to the city, although, prior to consolidation, the parish did help pay for fire protection in several of the rural fire protection districts. One district continues to provide fire protection in a rural area, but it is financed through a special fire protection district tax. Fire protection costs in the city and parish amounted to about $226 thousand per year in 1944-47 and increased to about $1,588 thousand per year in 1958-61, Table 9. Much of this increase can be attributed to expansion of the city limits to encompass an additional 30 square miles at time of consolidation. Before consolidation there were only five fire stations in operation and the fire-fighting equipment was quite inadequate. With the consolidation and expansion of city limits, more appropriate equipment was purchased, new fire hydrants installed, and the number of fire stations increased to thirteen plus a headquarters building. The improved service resulted in an improved fire insurance rating from Class III to Class II, the lowest rates of any city in Louisiana. The greatest share of the increased cost, however, can be attributed to the expanded program of inspections and instruction in fire prevention. The number of employees increased considerably as the city limits were extended.

About 85 per cent of the fire department's expense goes for salaries. This also includes employee benefits such as pensions, medical insurance, and hospitalization. Nevertheless, annual cost per capita in the city increased from $3.65 in 1944-47 to $6.83, in comparable dollars, for 1958-61. If the comparison is made on a parish-wide basis, without adjustment of dollar values, the annual costs in 1958-61 were $7.10 per capita. This was slightly higher than the $6.00 national average.[2]

Although fire protection costs have increased substantially since consolidation, there is a compensating advantage to homeowners through a reduction in fire insurance rates. Prior to consolidation, the City of Baton Rouge had a base fire insurance rate of $2.20 per thousand on residential property, while similar property, adjoining the city, had a rate of $5 per thousand. After applying the expanded fire protection program to include the annexed areas, the insurance rates for the newly added areas were reduced to the same rate as for the old city limits, and were later reduced city-wide to $1.60 per thousand for frame residences and $1.20 per thousand for brick dwellings.[3]

Police protection, as used in this context, refers to the city police function financially supported through the city budget. Police protection to non-city residents is provided by the sheriff's office, which is a constitutional office and not specifically dependent upon the city-parish budget for financial support. The city-parish budgets contributed about one-third of the total sheriff's office expenditures, both before and after consoldiation. The cost of police protection in the City of Baton Rouge averaged about $121 thousand per year in 1944-47. By 1958-61 the annual cost averaged about $1,603 thousand, Table 9. Here again, it must be remembered that the City annexed an additional 30 square miles at the time of consolidation in 1949. Nevertheless, annual per capita costs increased from $2.38 in 1944-47 to $6.78 in 1958-61, in comparable dollars, Table 26. With the expansion of city limits to encompass more than six times its preconsolidation area, it was inevitable that an enormous increase in the size of the police force would be necessary. Additional services were made available by establishing an auto theft bureau, a K-9 corps, and many new traffic patrols. As is true for the fire department, salaries and employee benefits make up about 85 per cent of the cost of the police department.

General Services is a category including traffic control, planning, license inspection, health services, library services, and recreation. Total expenditures for these services increased from about $78 thousand per year in 1944-47 to about $663 thousand per year in 1958-61. Emphasis upon the respective services within this group changed considerably over the fifteen-year interval. Traffic control and engineering costs increased at an enormous rate, as might well be expected from the rapid traffic build-up over a greatly expanded area. Some new services initiated after consolidation explain part of the increased costs. These include inoculations for prevention of disease, food inspection, and insect and pest control. The expansion of library services has also been impressive. An additional library, an increase from 16 to 52 employees, two bookmobiles, and an increase from 45,000 to 140,000 volumes, with a vastly improved circulation, explain the increase in cost of library service. Recreation expenditures, on the other hand, decreased because the recreation and park commission became a self-sufficient body after it was granted the authority by the state constitution to issue bonds and finance its own activities. Thus, the city and parish budgets provided, through special contributions, about three-fourths of the funds used by the recreation and park commission in 1944-47, but during 1958-61, this agency received no financial support from the city-parish budget.

The Department of Public Works is essentially the largest functional department of city-parish government. It is a consolidated agency serving both the city and parish. Its many and varied responsibilities are indicated by division titles such as engineering and construction, street maintenance, public building maintenance, central garage, sewer maintenance, refuse collection, and safety inspection. Expenditures for public works have grown at a rate that is somewhat slower than that of other departments. Expenditures in 1944-47 averaged about $701 thousand per year compared to $3,548 thousand per year in 1958-61, Table 9. Prior to consolidation, city expenditure for public works were about half as large as parish expenditures, but by 1958-61 the situation was almost reversed; city expenditures had risen to about $2,142 thousand compared to $1,406 thousand for the parish. Per capita costs for public works increased from $6.07 per year in 1944-47 to $10.29, in comparable dollars, for 1958-61. The rapid growth in public works is indicative of the popular demand for public improvements, particularly for streets, roads, and drainage. The increased cost rests primarily on the expansion of services for refuse collection, street lighting, and maintenance of streets, bridges, canals, sewers, and public buildings.

Capital Expenditures accounted for the largest share of the city-parish budget during 1944-47 but ranked fourth in 1958-61. In the earlier period, capital expenditures amounted to $705 thousand in contrast to $1,407 thousand during the latter period, Table 9. The 1944-47 audits did not identify capital expenditures as to ultimate use, but for 1958-61 it was noted that 56 per cent of the city capital expenditures occurred through the department of public works, with one-third going for drainage and about one-fifth for streets. New equipment for the department accounted for about 30 per cent of the expenditures by the department of public works. In the parish budget, about 67 per cent of the capital expenditures went to the department of public works in 1958-61. The allocation of this portion of expenditures showed about 37 per cent for streets, 27 per cent for new equipment, and 32 per cent for drainage and engineering. On a per capita basis, and in constant dollars, capital expenditures for the entire parish decreased from $6.10 in 1944-47 to $4.09 in 1958-61.

Contributions to Constitutional Offices

As was mentioned previously, the constitutional offices remained in effect after the consolidation and, as was customary in the past, the city and parish continued to contribute toward the support of constitutional offices, Figure XVIII. In 1944-47, the total annual contribution by the entire parish was about $142 thousand. By 1958-61, the amount had increased to about $770 thousand, Table 9. City contributions to constitutional offices were relatively insignificant for 1944-47, but by 1958-61 amounted to about $150 thousand annually. Contributions went primarily to the sheriff's office which accounted for 50 per cent, and the family court received 32 per cent. Parish-wide contributions to constitutional offices amounted to 96 cents per capita per year in 1944-47 and $1.72 in 1958-61, in comparable dollars.

A large part of the increased contribution to the sheriff's office is explained by the increased cost of maintaining prisoners. Not only had the costs for care, feeding, and transportation increased, but the number of prisoners more than doubled over the fifteen-year period. The appreciable increase in costs for the clerk of court

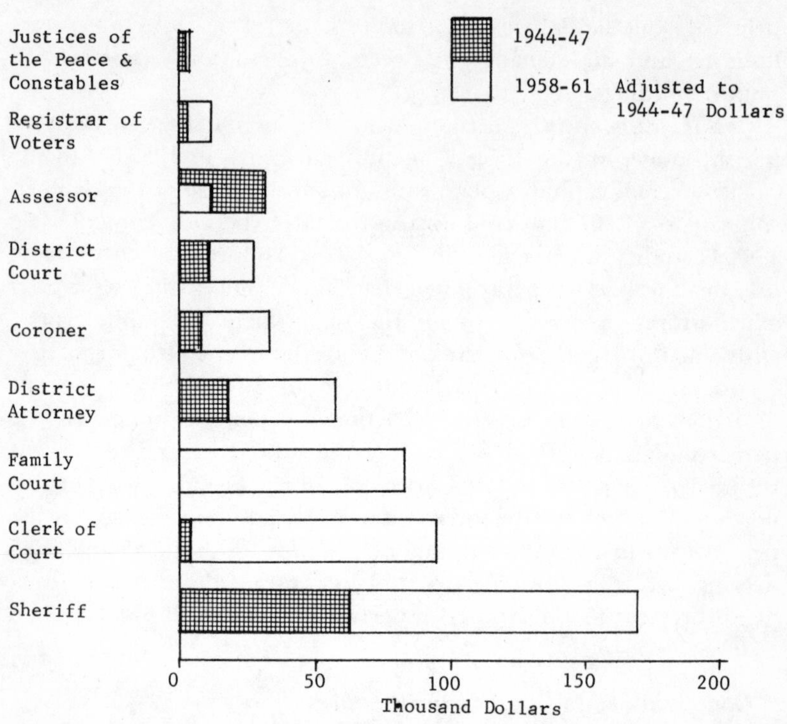

FIGURE XVIII Financial Support Given by Local Government to Parish Constitutional Offices, Before (1944-47) and After (1958-61) Consolidation, East Baton Rouge Parish

rests mainly on the tremendous increase in volume of legal transactions and efforts to improve filing of official records through photostats and use of microfilm. The parish contributed about four times more than the city in support of constitutional offices. Here again, the sheriff's office received the greater portion, about 43 per cent of the total contributions to constitutional offices in 1944-47, and 30 per cent in 1958-61. During this latter period, the clerk of court, family court, and district attorney received 24, 13, and 14 per cent of the total contributions to constitutional offices, respectively.

Contributions to Other Agencies accounted for about 4 per cent of the total budget in 1944-47 and slightly less than 1 per cent in 1958-61.[4] The average annual dollar volume allocated for this purpose was about $81 thousand in 1944-47 and $98 thousand in 1958-61.

Percentage of Expenditures by Type of Service

The department of public works and capital improvements together accounted for about two-thirds of both city and parish expenditures in 1944-47. Both declined in relative importance by 1958-61 to 40 and 60 per cent, respectively, Table 10. City expendi-

TABLE 10
Percentage of Total Expenditures by Type of Service, East Baton Rouge Parish, 1944-47 and 1958-61

Service	City 1944-47	City 1958-61	Parish 1944-47	Parish 1958-61	City and Parish 1944-47	City and Parish 1958-61
Legislative & Executive	0.9%	0.2%	0.5%	1.4%	0.7%	0.6%
Judicial	0.9	0.8	1.7	1.5	1.3	1.0
Contributions to other Agencies	5.1	0.8	2.3	1.2	3.7	0.9
Contributions to Constitutional offices	0.1	2.0	13.3	18.4	6.6	7.2
General Services	1.5	6.7	5.8	5.3	3.6	6.3
Administration	3.2	2.6	2.3	7.1	2.8	4.1
Employee Benefits	-	3.2	-	4.4	-	3.6
Police Protection	11.0	21.9	-	-	5.6	14.8
Fire Protection	14.2	21.8	6.6	-	10.5	15.0
Capital Expenditures	41.9	10.6	23.2	18.9	32.7	13.2
Dept. of Public Works	21.2	29.4	44.3	41.8	32.5	33.3
TOTAL	100.0	100.0	100.0	100.0	100.0	100.0

tures for fire protection and police protection were next in importance with each accounting for 22 per cent in 1958-61. These had increased from 14 and 11 per cent, respectively, in 1944-47. Other departmental expenditures were of lesser importance, but parish contributions to constitutional offices have ranged from 13 to 18 per cent of total parish expenditures. Surprisingly enough, the city-parish legislative and executive share of expenditures is less than one per cent of the total. In fact, the percentage of total expenditures for the legislative and executive, judicial, contributions to other agencies, and capital expenditures, all decreased after the consolidation, while the share going for fire protection, police protection, public works, administration, general services, employee benefits and contributions to constitutional offices all increased.

Sources of Revenue

City

In the City of Baton Rouge, the annual general fund revenues during 1944-47 averaged about $664,000. Of this amount, almost half was derived from property taxes, about 30 per cent from licenses and permits, and 9 per cent from rents, concessions, and commissions, Table 29. Less than 2 per cent resulted from state aid. By 1958-61 the total revenues were over $7 million, with property taxes accounting for only 28 per cent; licenses and permits, 13 per cent; and rents, concessions, and commissions, less than one per cent. State aid, on the other hand, increased in importance to 12 per cent; and sales tax revenues provided the largest share – 36 per cent of the total city revenues, Figure XIX. The sales tax is credited with making expanded services possible without placing an oppressive burden on property owners.

Parish

East Baton Rouge Parish had general fund revenues of about $1 million per year during the period 1944-47. Of this amount, property taxes contributed about 45 per cent; state aid accounted for 23 per cent; and licenses and permits provided about 12 per cent. By 1958-61, the total revenues slightly exceeded $4 million. Property taxes and state aid retained the same position of importance as before, but sales tax revenues were introduced to replace other incidental contributions and actually accounted for 22 per cent of the Parish revenues, Figure XIX.

City-Parish

Looking at the combined revenues of the city and parish, one can see that general fund revenue needs expanded from $1.7 million in 1944-47 to $11.4 million in 1958-61, Table 31. The property tax is still the largest single source of revenue, although it decreased in importance from 47 per cent in 1944-47 to 33 per cent in 1958-61. The sales tax bolstered lagging revenues from other incidental sources. It accounted for 31 per cent of the total revenues in 1958-61, and was the direct result of a one per cent sales tax. State aid

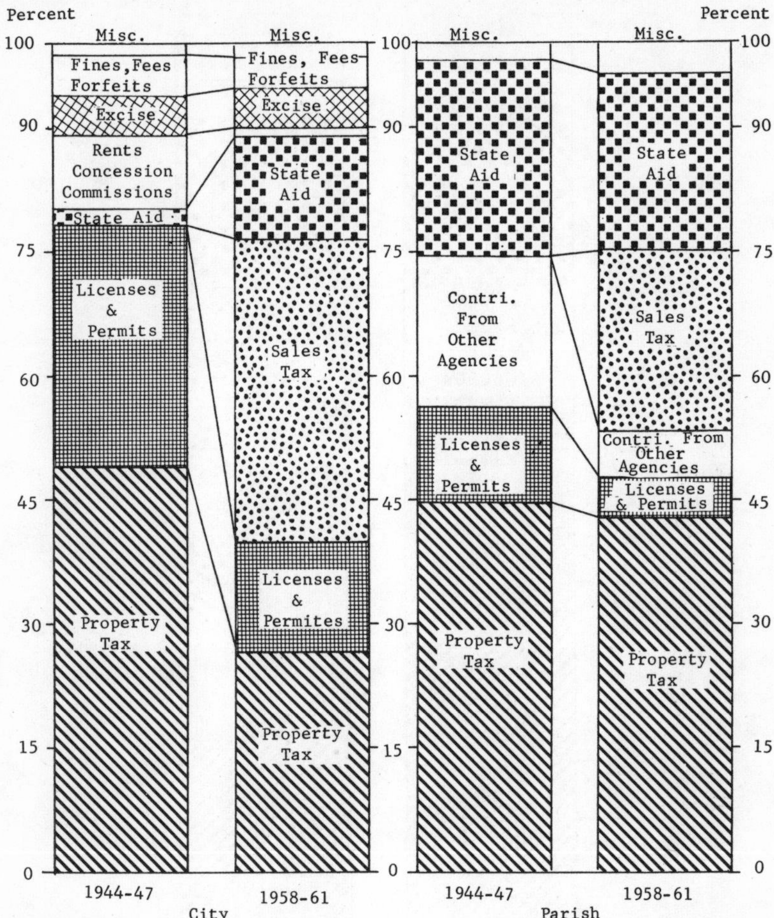

FIGURE XIX Proportion of Revenues Received from Various Sources, City of Baton Rouge and East Baton Rouge Parish, 1944-47 and 1958-61

continued to represent about 15 per cent of total revenues during both periods, Figure XX.

State aid moneys are derived primarily from special taxes collected by the state and ultimately distributed to parishes on a prorata basis. The severance tax, for example, as applied to forests and minerals, provided an average annual revenue to the parish of about $13,649 in 1944-47. The severance revenues for 1958-61 averaged only $11,423. (Some severance tax revenues are also paid to

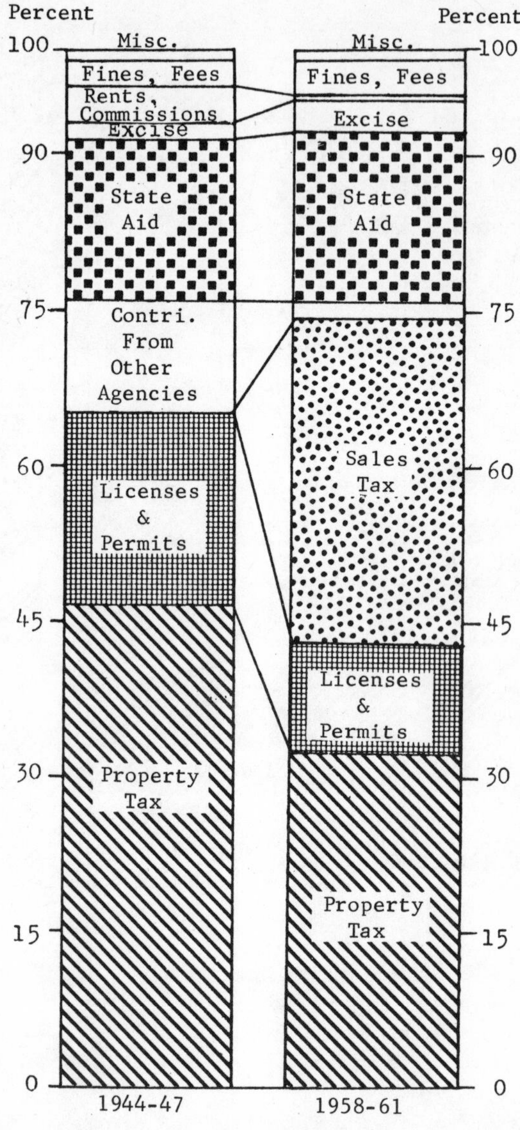

FIGURE XX Proportion of Revenues Received from Various Sources, City and Parish, 1944-47 and 1958-61

special districts, but these are not included with general revenues.) The gasoline tax was a far more important source of revenue in that it provided an average of $220,854 per year in 1944-47 and increased to $725,856 per year in 1958-61. Surprisingly, the tobacco tax contributed even more than the gasoline tax, but it went to the city. It averaged $771,775 per year during 1958-61, but tobacco taxes were not yet dedicated to local government in 1944-47. Special state grants, primarily for highway use, averaged more than $96,000 per year during 1958-61. The beer tax in 1958-61 yielded an average of $22,615 per year to the parish, and $103,235 per year to the city, Table 32. The chain store tax contributed an annual average of $3,830 to the parish in 1944-47 and increased to $4,900 per year in 1958-61. It was considerably more rewarding for the city in that it contributed about $14,150 per year during 1958-61.

Number of Property Taxpayers

The number of property taxpayers (including public utilities) listed on local tax rolls increased from a yearly average of 27,615 in 1944-47 to an average of 62,264 in 1958-61, Table 11. This repre-

TABLE 11
Number of Taxpayers, Including Public Utilities, in the Rural, City, and Industrial Areas of East Baton Rouge Parish

	Number of Taxpayers			
Year	Parish	Rural	City	Industrial Area
1944	24,200	17,722	6,478	
1945	25,966	19,229	6,737	*
1946	28,240	21,228	7,012	
1947	32,052	24,557	7,495	
Average	27,615	20,684	6,931	
1958	58,182	19,950	38,112	120
1959	60,669	20,876	39,676	117
1960	64,060	23,497	40,451	112
1961	66,145	25,096	40,941	108
Average	62,264	22,355	39,795	114

*Industrial area not differentiated 1944-47.

sents an increase of 125 per cent, whereas population increased only slightly, from an average of 20,684 in 1944-47 to 22,355 in 1958-61. The number in the city, however, increased from 6,931 to 39,795. Most of this large increase to the city and slight increase to the rural area is explained by the expansion of the city limits at the time of the city-parish consolidation. The number of public utilities paying property taxes are far more prevalent in the rural and industrial areas than in the city. An average of 17 public utilities were paying property taxes in the city during 1944-47, and this number dropped to 16 during 1958-61. Outside the city, public utilities numbered 113 during 1944-47 and only 83 during 1958-61. A total of 86 industries were listed in the tax rolls as operating in the industrial areas during the period 1958-61, Table 12.

TABLE 12

Number of Public Utilities, and Industries in Industrial Areas, on the Tax Rolls in East Baton Rouge Parish, 1944-47 and 1958-61

Year	Public Utilities			Industries in
	City	Rural	Industrial	Industrial Areas
1944	14	116		
1945	17	113		
1946	17	114		
1947	19	111	*	*
Average	17	113		
1958	15	45	36	84
1959	16	58	28	89
1960	16	58	24	88
1961	16	58	24	84
Average	16	55	28	86

*Industrial areas not differentiated 1944-47.

Special Districts

Special districts are frequently created to permit the financing of public services to specific areas. The costs are theoretically borne by taxpayers receiving the benefit of these special services. A municipality is almost like a special district because, as a public corporation, it has the privilege of undertaking public projects and devising means of providing for their financial support. In 1944-47, only three types of special districts of any consequence were in East Baton Rouge Parish: sewerage, drainage, and road districts. Those within the city limits were continued as constituted prior to consolidation until the purpose for which they were established was completed. The road districts were finally discontinued and the construction and maintenance of city streets and parish roads became a responsibility of the department of public works. Special districts, particularly for garbage collection and road lighting, have emerged at a rapid rate since the consolidation. These are providing weird patterns of public service areas in suburban developments surrounding the city, Figures XXI and XXII.

The eight mill city tax provided about $1.5 million annual revenues to Baton Rouge in 1958-61. The Town of Zachary and the Town of Baker had corresponding figures of $12,000 and $39,000, respectively. The Scotlandville fire protection district revenues amounted to about $55,000 during the same period. The special hospital district in the Baker-Zachary area, with a 2.50 mill tax rate, derived annual revenues averaging $64,194 in 1958-61, Figure XXIII. Although the eight mill city tax in Baton Rouge provides for the bulk of city services, a few special districts still function within the city limits—sewer districts and a few road lighting districts, for example. The cost of services provided through special districts are readily apparent in their special millage rates. The two sewer districts carried on the tax rolls in 1961 had rates of 0.75 mills and 2.90 mills, respectively. Garbage district rates ranged from 2.50 to 5.00 mills, with an average of 4.05 mills. Road lighting districts ranged from 2.50 to 5.00 mills, with 20 of the 24 districts having the 5.00 mill rate. The hospital district had a rate of 2.50 mills, the levee district a rate of 4.00 mills, the Scotlandville fire protection district a high of 8.50 mills. The towns of Baker and Zachary had millage rates of 13.00 and 6.00, respectively, Figure XXIV. Part of the high cost of special services may be attributed to the tendency of each district to oversubscribe the financing of these services, with the end result that revenues invariably exceed expenditures, as observed every year for the period 1958-61, Table 34. From a business standpoint, this is better than operating at a

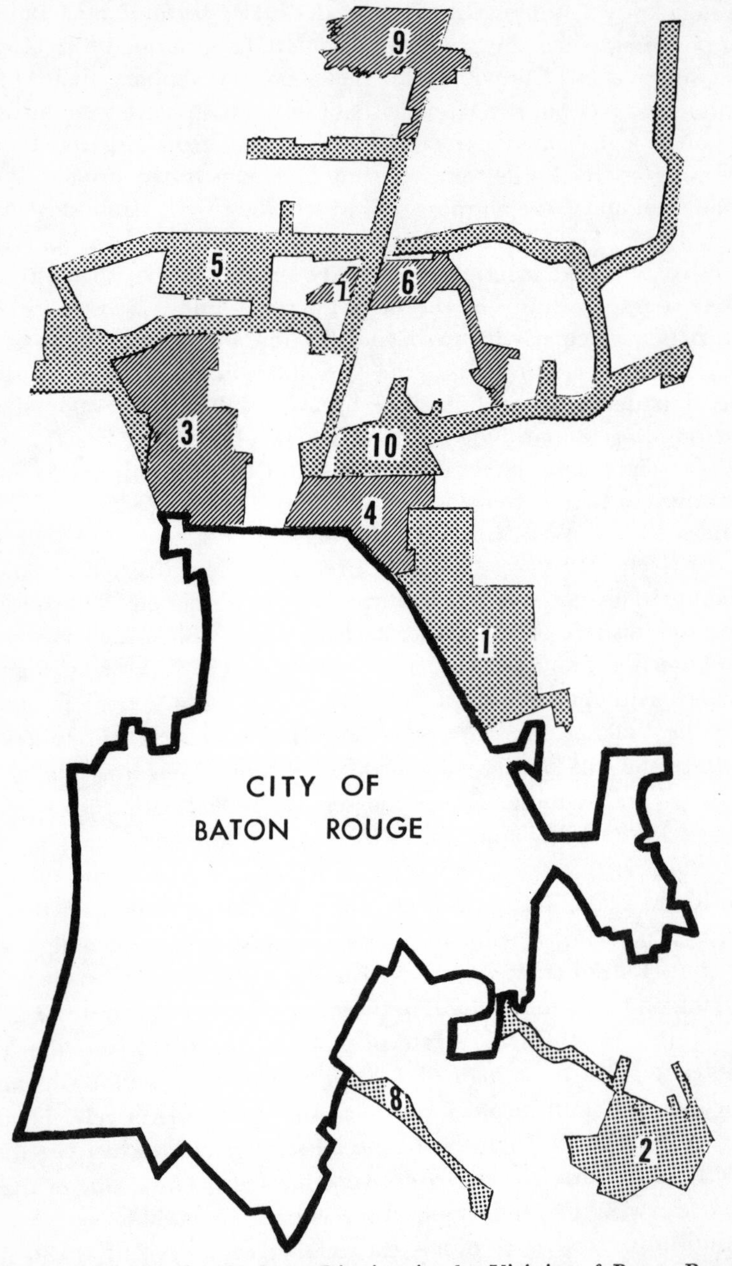

FIGURE XXI Special Garbage Districts in the Vicinity of Baton Rouge, 1961

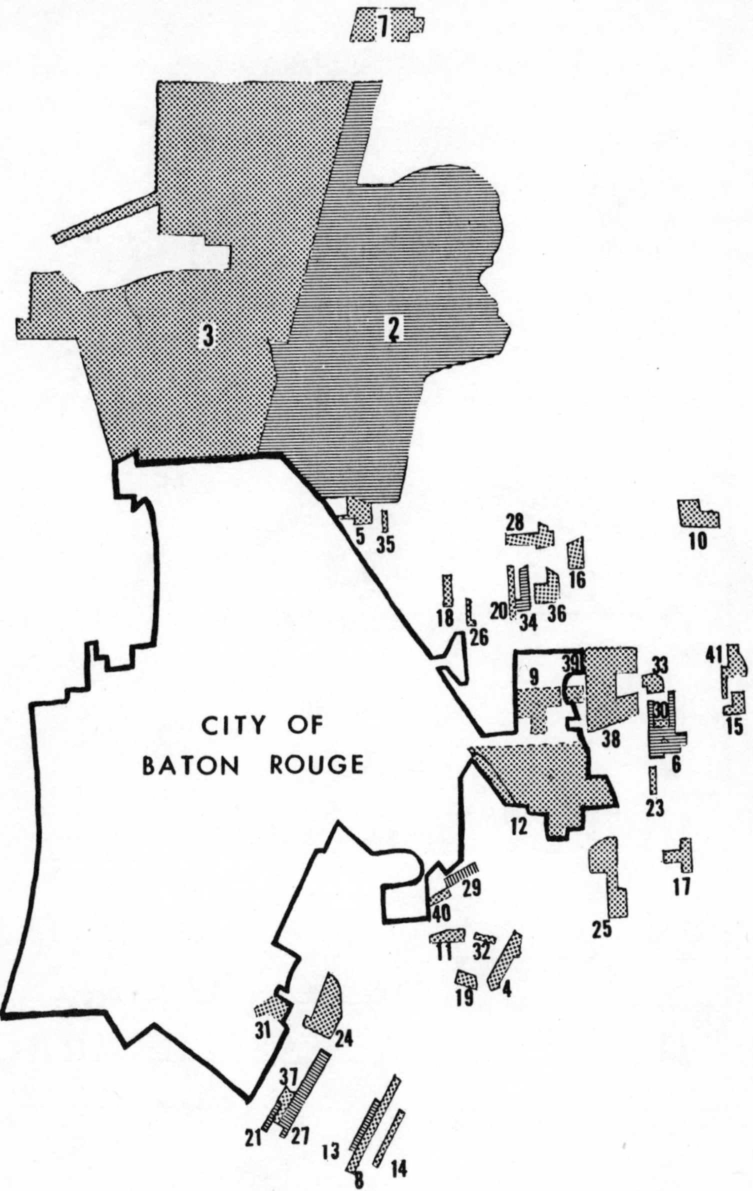

FIGURE XXII The Many Special Road Lighting Districts Surrounding Baton Rouge

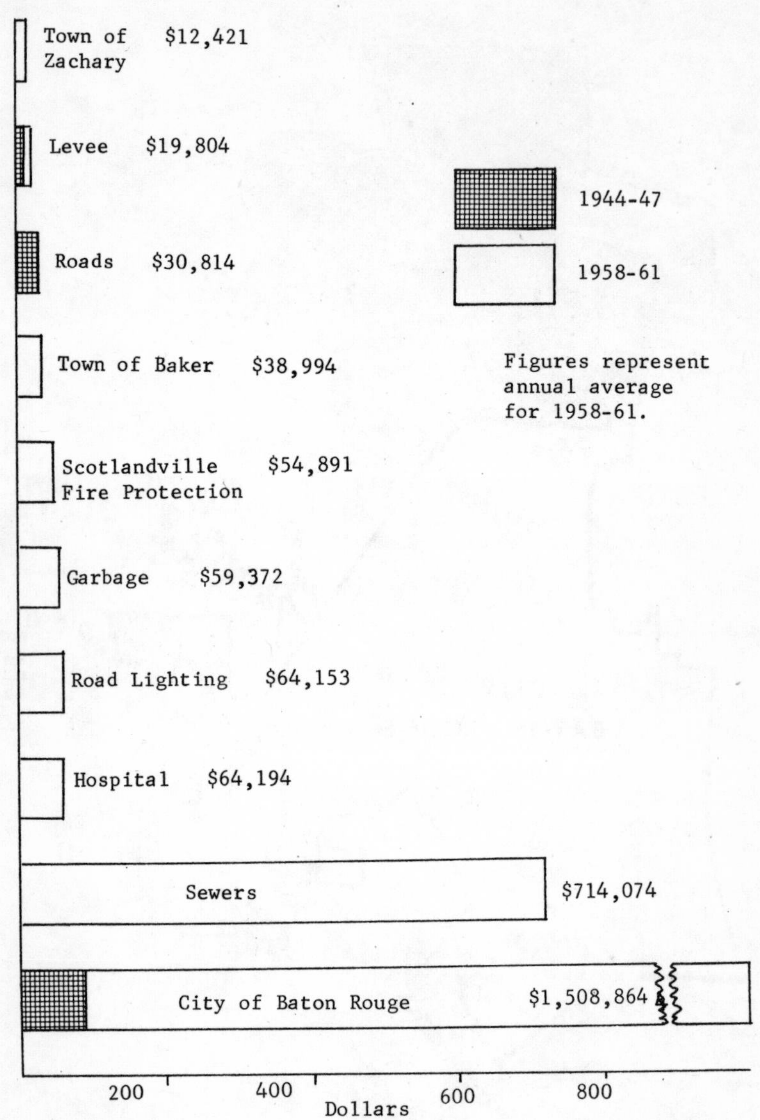

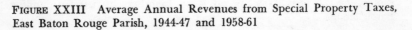

FIGURE XXIII Average Annual Revenues from Special Property Taxes, East Baton Rouge Parish, 1944-47 and 1958-61

State Tax, 5¾ Mills		$
Parish-wide Taxes		
Parish Tax 4.00		
General School 5.00		
School-Maintenance 5.00		
School-Bond & Coupon 11.50	28.60 Mills	
Spl. Sch. M.E.F. 1.00		
Recreation-Bond .60		
Recreation-Tax 1.00		
Courthouse .50		
City of Baton Rouge, 8.00 Mills		
Consolidated Sewer No. 1, 2.90 Mills		
Sewer District No. 6-A, .75 Mills		
Garbage District No. 1, 3.50 Mills		
Garbage District No. 2, 3.50 Mills		
Garbage District No. 3, 3.00 Mills		
Garbage District No. 4, 5.00 Mills		
Garbage District No. 5, 2.50 Mills		
Garbage District No. 6, 4.00 Mills		
Garbage District No. 7, 4.50 Mills		
Garbage District No. 8, 5.00 Mills		
Garbage District No. 9, 4.50 Mills		
Garbage District No. 10, 5.00 Mills		
Road Lighting No. 2 & 3, 5.00 Mills		
Road Lighting No. 4 & 9, 5.00 Mills		
Road Lighting No. 10 & 13, 5.00 Mills		
Road Lighting No. 5, 3.00 Mills		
Road Lighting No. 6, 2.50 Mills		
Road Lighting No. 8, 2.50 Mills		
Road Lighting No. 14 & 16, 5.00 Mills		
Road Lighting No. 18 & 19, 5.00 Mills		
Road Lighting No. 11, 3.00 Mills		
Road Lighting No. 12, 3.00 Mills		
Road Lighting No. 20 & 21, 5.00 Mills		
Road Lighting No. 24 & 25, 5.00 Mills		
Road Lighting No. 26 & 28, 5.00 Mills		
Road Lighting No. 29, 5.00 Mills		
Hosp. Dist. No. 1, 2.50 Mills		
Acreage Tax, 2c Per Acre		
Levee District, 4.00 Mills		
Scotland Fire Prot., 8.50 Mills		
Town of Baker, 13.00 Mills		
Town of Zachary, 6.00 Mills		
Interest on Taxes		
Cost		
TOTAL		$

FIGURE XXIV Property Tax Millage Rates for State, Parish, and City Taxes, 1961 deficit, but a gradual reduction in millage rates might be warranted in some districts.

Assessments and Taxation

The consolidation had no direct effect on property assessments; that is, assessment policies did not change. Many new properties, however, created new values. The total assessed value of property in East Baton Rouge Parish increased from an annual average of $163,549,768 in 1944-47 to $428,979,778 in 1958-61. This signifies an increase of 162 per cent over a fifteen-year period. An attempt to compare assessed values by taxing districts is difficult because the 1949 consolidation resulted in expanded city limits and also newly designated industrial areas. Nevertheless, it is possible to compare the rate of assessment growth from year to year, for rural, city, and industrial divisions of the parish. The average annual rate of growth in assessments during 1944-47 was 4.94 per cent for city properties and 5.38 per cent for rural properties. For 1958-61, however, the average annual increase in assessments was 4.17 per cent for the city and 12.51 per cent for the rural area. During this latter period, the industrial area was given individual recognition and showed a 10.5 per cent increase in assessed value from 1958 to 1959, but a decrease of 1.2 and 0.1 per cent, respectively, for the next two years. Changes in assessed values by taxing districts are shown in Figure XXV.

At the same time that total assessment values were increasing in the city and parish, the total millage rates were also increasing. The parish-wide millage rate increased from 10.36 mills for 1944-47 to 28.50 in 1958-61. This represents an increase of 175 per cent. Likewise, the city millage increased from 1.8 in 1944-47 to 7.9 in 1958-61, or an increase of 339 per cent, Table 13.

Assessment per Taxpayer

The average assessed value per taxpayer was changed considerably by the redesignation of taxing districts. Whereas the industrial areas and most of the suburban developments were considered part of the rural area in 1944-47, by 1949 the industrial areas were designated as separate taxing districts and the city had expanded its limits to engulf an additional 30 square miles of fringe residential areas. These changes largely explain the reduction in assessed value per rural taxpayer and the increase in assessment per city taxpayer.

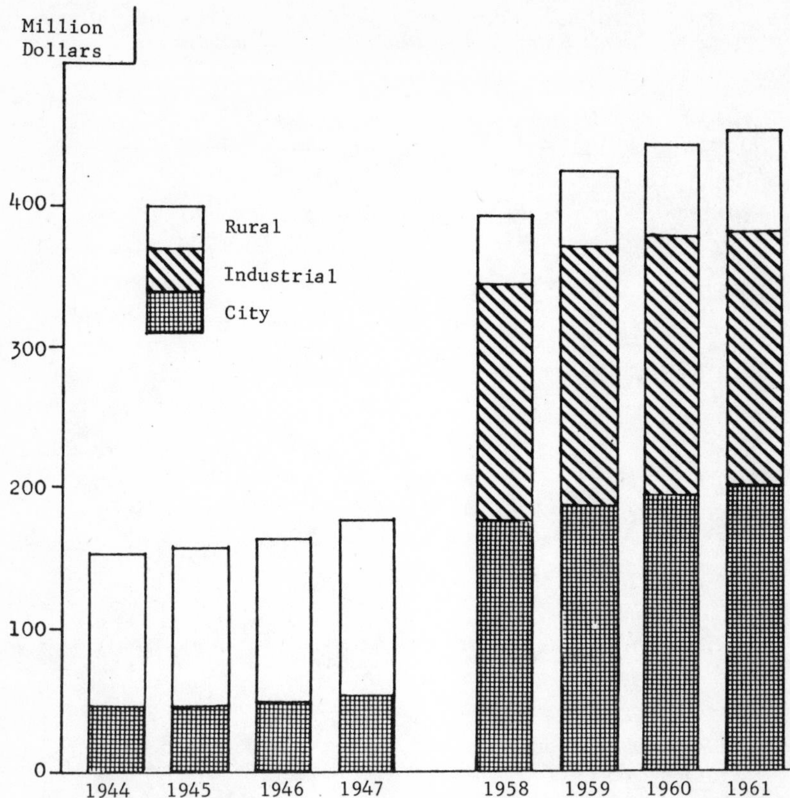

FIGURE XXV Assessed Value of City, Rural, and Industrial Property, East Baton Rouge Parish, 1944-47 and 1958-61

The average assessed value per taxpayer in East Baton Rouge Parish in 1944-47 was $5,896. By 1958-61, the average had increased to $6,890, Table 14. During the latter period, the average per rural taxpayer was $2,640, compared to $4,815 per city taxpayer, and $1,561,964 per industry. On a parish-wide basis assessed valuation increased 162 per cent from 1944-47 to 1958-61.

Acreage Assessed

The approximate land area of the parish is 295,680 acres,[5] of which 80 per cent is on the assessment rolls as assessed acreage. The remaining area is taken up in highways, residential lots, waterways, etc. The average number of acres assessed annually in 1958-61

TABLE 13

General Millage Rates Paid by Rural and City Taxpayers, 1944-47 and 1958-61

Year	Tax Rate* Parish-Wide	City Only
	Mills	
1944	9.32	1.8
1945	10.82	1.8
1946	10.80	1.8
1947	10.52	1.8
Average	10.36	1.8
1958	26.40	7.5
1959	30.60	8.0
1960	28.50	8.0
1961	28.60	8.0
Average	28.50	7.9

*Excludes millage rates applied to special districts and the 5.75 mill state tax.

TABLE 14

Average Assessed Value per Taxpayer in City, Rural, and Industrial Areas of East Baton Rouge Parish, 1944-47 and 1958-61

	Average Assessed Value per Taxpayer			
Year	Parish	Rural	City	Industrial
1944	$6,360	$6,203	$6,788	
1945	5,833	5,799	5,919	
1946	5,800	5,484	6,757	
1947	5,591	5,229	6,777	
Average	5,896	5,679+	6,560	
1958	6,783	2,465	4,704	$1,385,060
1959	7,029	2,585	4,757	1,570,184
1960	6,894	2,725	4,849	1,619,880
1961	6,852	2,785	4,950	1,672,730
Average	6,890	2,640	4,815	1,561,964

*Industrial area not differentiated 1944-47.

+Includes value of industrial property not included in corresponding average for 1958-61.

was 3,968 in the City of Baton Rouge, 3,080 in the industrial areas, and 207,690 in the remainder of the parish, Table 15. The

TABLE 15

Acreage Assessed in City, Rural, and Industrial Areas of East Baton Rouge Parish, 1944-47 and 1958-61

	Assessed Acreage			
Year	City	Rural	Industrial	Total Parish
1944	126.10	264,631.20		264,757.30
1945	125.10	258,489.82	*	258,614.92
1946	185.00	263,784.80		263,969.80
1947	258.56	262,608.16		262,866.72
Average	173.69	262,378.51		262,552.20
1958	4,057.53	214,030.14	3,071.80	221,159.47
1959	3,641.24	201,940.42	3,084.29	208,665.95
1960	3,330.28	186,929.09	3,084.29	193,343.66
1961	4,844.75	227,862.00+	3,081.23	235,787.98
Average 1958-61	3,968.45	207,690.41	3,080.40	214,739.26

*Industrial area not differentiated 1944-47.

+Approximately 40,000 acres of pasture land added to assessment rolls in 1961.

TABLE 16

Average Assessed Value of Farmland, East Baton Rouge Parish, 1946 and 1960

	Assessment per Acre*	
	1946	1960
Land Only	$18	$18
Land and Improvements	28	38

*Based on 20 per cent sample of rural properties more than one acre in size and including all land in each sample tract, that is, pasture, woodland, etc.

average assessed value of rural farm land in 1960 was exactly the same as its value in 1946; that is, $18.00 per acre. Table 16. The value of improvements, however, did show an increase of $10.00 per acre over the fifteen-year period. This, undoubtedly, resulted from new improvements. Farmland taxes per acre, including improvements thereon, averaged 42 cents per year in 1944-47 and $1.31 in 1958-61.[6]

Homestead Exemption

The Louisiana Homestead Exemption Law, which came into being during the depression of the 1930's, still continues to exempt owner-occupied homesteads from property taxes on assessed values up to $2,000. The law provides:

> . . . exemption from State, parish and special taxes, on a tract of land, or two or more tracts of land with a residence on one tract and a field, pasture or garden on the other tract or tracts, not exceeding one hundred and sixty acres, buildings and appurtenances, whether rural or urban, owned and occupied by every head of a family, or person having a mother or father, or a person or persons dependent on him or her for support, to the value of Two Thousand Dollars; provided that this exemption shall not extend to any municipal or city taxes . . . and the State Treasurer shall be authorized and is directed to reimburse the general or special funds of the State and any of its political subdivisions . . . out of funds which shall be established and provided for by the Legislature in the Property Tax Relief Fund. . . .[7]

A higher exemption of $5,000 is extended to veterans of World War II and of the Korean War. The veterans' exemption is for a five-year period, with a possibility of a ten-year exemption for a veteran of both wars. The exemption is scheduled to terminate in 1964 for World War II veterans and in 1969 for veterans of the Korean War. Exemptions apply to most state and local property taxes, with the exception of city and special district taxes. The tax revenues on exempted values, however, are not lost to the local government, but are reimbursed through the state property tax relief fund. This fund is maintained by state taxes on income, alcoholic beverages, and other sources. Of the total assessed values for the city and rural areas of the parish, the portion that was covered by homestead and veterans exemption averaged about 13 per cent for the combined city and rural areas during the period 1944-47. But by 1958-61, the homestead exemptions in the city had increased to about one-fourth of the total assessed value, and exemptions in the rural area averaged 41 per cent of the total assesed value. On a parish-wide basis the exemption accounted for

TABLE 17

Proportion of Assessed Value Covered by Homestead and Veterans Exemptions, East Baton Rouge Parish, Rural and City, 1944-47 and 1958-61

Year	Homestead Exempt Parish	Rural	City
1944	10.63%	9.77%	12.76%
1945	12.07	11.67	13.05
1946	13.21	13.17	13.34
1947	15.15	15.60	14.04
Average 1944-47	12.76	12.55	13.30
1958	29.30	42.34	26.15
1959	29.54	40.11	26.51
1960	29.11	40.48	25.39
1961	28.66	40.37	24.62
Average* 1958-61	29.16	40.82	25.66

*Separate classification of the industrial area and extension of city limits after 1949 accounts for much of the observed increase in 1958-61.

about 29 per cent of the total parish assessment, Table 17. Taxes extended through homestead and veterans exemption represent the amount of property taxes whose burden has been shifted from the property owners to all taxpayers contributing to the state property tax relief fund. In 1944-47 taxes extended in East Baton Rouge Parish by the exemption, amounted to an annual average of $403,753. By 1958-61, these tax exemptions averaged $2,715,869 per year, Table 18.

Industrial Exemption

In addition to the homestead and veterans exemptions offered to homeowners, an industrial exemption is offered to new and expanding industries which provides for exemption from payment of property taxes for a period of ten years (an initial five-year exemption plus a five-year renewal, subject to compliance with terms of contract). The ten-year property tax exemption was provided by Legislative Act 401 in 1946. It authorized the state board of commerce

TABLE 18

Assessed Value and Taxes Extended Through Homestead and Veterans Exemptions, East Baton Rouge Parish, Excluding Special District Taxes

Year	Total Assessments*	Assessed Value Covered by Exemption	Taxes Extended by Exemption
1944	$153,907,041	$16,354,785	$292,893.22
1945	157,301,485	18,993,405	363,709.82
1946	163,781,825	21,643,160	412,765.01
1947	179,208,724	27,158,440	545,644.32
Average 1944-47	$163,549,768	$21,037,448	$403,753.09
1958	$228,461,433	$66,960,005	$2,254,954.23
1959	242,706,315	71,686,125	2,797,299.92
1960	260,196,040	75,732,665	2,799,545.50
1961	272,555,110	78,116,995	3,011,677.13
Average 1958-61	$250,979,725	$73,123,947	$2,715,869.19

*Excludes Industrial Area 1958-61.

and industry, with the approval of the governor, to contract with the owner of any new manufacturing establishment in the state or with the owner of an addition or additions to any manufacturing establishments already existing in the state, for the exemption from taxation of any such new manufacturing establishment or addition upon such terms and conditions as the board, with the approval of the governor, may deem to be the best interests of the state.

The terms "manufacturing establishment" and "addition or additions" as used in this paragraph mean a new plant or establishment or an addition to any existing plant or establishment which engages in the business of working raw materials into wares suitable for use or which gives new shapes, new qualities or new combinations to matter which has already gone through some artificial process. No exemption shall be contracted for any new manufacturing establishment in any locality where there is a manufacturing establishment actually engaged in the manufacture of the same or closely competitive articles without the written consent of the owner of such existing manufacturing establishment to be attached to and identified with the contract of exemption. No exemption from taxes shall be granted under the authority of this paragraph for a longer initial period than five (5) calendar years succeeding the date of any such contract; provided, that upon application within ninety (90) days before the expiration of the initial period of five (5) years, and upon proper showing of a full compliance with the contract of exemption by the contractee, any exemption granted under the authority of this paragraph shall be renewed for an additional period of five (5) calendar years. Any such exemption shall ipso facto cease upon violation of the terms and conditions of the contract which granted the same....

All property exempted in accordance with the provisions of this Section shall be valued at actual cash value, listed on the assessment rolls and submitted to the Louisiana Tax Commission, but no taxes shall be collected thereon during the period of exemption. On January 1st following the expiration of any contract of exemption entered into under this Section, all property exempted by any such contract shall be valued at actual cash value, listed on the assessment rolls and all taxes imposed upon the same shall be assessed and collected in the manner provided by law.[8]

During the period 1944-47, the assessed value of manufacturing plants under ten-year tax exemption contracts was $75,121,609. By 1958-61 the assessed value of plants or portion of plants covered by the industrial tax exemption averaged $352,499,207 per year, Table 19.

Other Exemptions

As is customary in other states, all public property and the many religious, charitable, and educational institutions are tax exempt. These include: places of worship, rectories, parsonages, and places of burial; lodges and clubs organized for and practicing charitable and fraternal purposes; schools and colleges; and nonprofit athletic or physical culture clubs with an active membership of not less than one thousand, holding, in equipped gymnasiums, physical development classes open daily to all members under supervision of regular physical directors, with juvenile and junior classes, and promoting physical and health development in all ages above eight years. The exemption extends only to property and grounds used for these purposes, and not leased for profit or income.

Electric cooperatives are assessed, although they are exempt from all taxes for a period of twenty-five years succeeding their completion. This includes assessment on highlines, transmission lines, and distribution lines of electric cooperatives organized and doing business pursuant to the rural electrification act of congress, as amended. Other properties such as moneys, credits, household goods,

TABLE 19

Value and Nature of Exempt Property, East Baton Rouge Parish, 1944-47 and 1958-61

Year	Total Assessments Including Fully Exempt Property	Manufacturing Plants Under Ten-Year Contract	Charitable, Public, Educational, etc.	Total Exemption	Exempt as Per cent of Total
	Dollars				Per cent
1944	229,028,650	75,121,609	-	75,121,609	32.80
1945	232,423,094	75,121,609	-	75,121,609	32.32
1946	258,296,088	75,121,609	19,392,654	94,514,263	36.59
1947	274,411,253	75,121,609	20,080,920	95,202,529	34.69
Average 1944-47	248,539,771	75,121,609	-	84,990,002	34.10
1958	805,353,966	383,449,266	27,236,060	410,685,326	51.00
1959	786,223,196	333,206,586	26,598,730	359,805,316	45.76
1960	815,908,776	341,529,031	32,757,095	374,286,126	45.87
1961	841,066,126	351,811,946	36,044,240	387,856,186	46.11
Average 1958-61	812,138,016	352,499,207	30,659,031	383,158,238	47.18

motor vehicles, agricultural products, and civic enterprises are not only exempt from taxation, but are not currently assessed in East Baton Rouge Parish. The assessed value of this group of "other exemptions" averaged $30,659,031 per year during 1958-61.

A combined total of the charitable and industrial exemptions reveals that they accounted for about one-third of the total assessed property values in the parish during 1944-47 and about 47 per cent in 1958-61. This implies that almost one-half of the assessed property value in the parish is exempt from taxation entirely, and an additional one-fourth of the assessed value of nonindustrial property qualifies for homestead and veterans exemption. Of course, there is a difference in so far as local revenues are concerned; the industrial and charitable exemptions cancel the tax obligation, hence tax revenues from those sources are lost to the parish; but taxes due on homestead and veterans exemptions are collected from the state property tax relief fund instead of from the individual property owners.

Property Taxes Per Taxpayer

Without differentiating between rural and city taxpayers, the tax load to each taxpayer in East Baton Rouge Parish for the period 1944-47 averaged $61.08 per year. In 1958-61, the average was $196.36. Of these respective amounts, about 47 per cent of the tax in 1944-47 was used in the city and parish general funds, compared to about 25 per cent during 1958-61. Based upon the proportion of assessment that is homestead exempt (including veterans exemption), the state property tax relief fund paid almost 30 per cent of the taxpayers property tax bill in 1958-61, compared to about 13 per cent in 1944-47.

Rural Taxpayers

Property taxes per rural taxpayer averaged $58.83 per year during the period 1944-47. Of this amount, about 30 per cent went to the city-parish general fund and the other 70 per cent for schools and courthouse maintenance. Based upon the proportion of assessed value classified as homestead exempt at that time, it is estimated that a little more than $7.00 of the individual taxpayers bill was paid by the state through the property tax relief fund, Table 20.

In 1958-61 the average property tax load per rural taxpayer amounted to $75.24 and about 45 per cent of this was allocated to the city-parish general fund. The other 55 per cent was dedicated to schools, recreation, and courthouse maintenance. The homestead and veterans exemption during this period averaged about $31.00 per rural taxpayer. Thus, by virtue of this exemption, the state paid about 40 per cent of the property tax bill for rural taxpayers.

City Taxpayers. Property taxes per city taxpayer averaged $79.77 per year during the period 1944-47. About three-fourths of this tax was allocated to the city-parish general fund and the balance to schools and courthouse maintenance. By 1958-61 the tax load per city taxpayer had increased to $175.27, of which only about one-third was allocated to the city-parish general fund and two-thirds to schools, recreation, and courthouse maintenance, Table 20. Homestead and veterans exemption per city taxpayer averaged about $45.00 per year during the period 1958-61; thus the state property tax relief fund paid about one-fourth of the property tax bill for city taxpayers.

TABLE 20

Average Annual Assessment, Millage Rate, and Property Taxes per Taxpayer, 1944-47 and 1958-61

	Rural		City	
	1944-47	1958-61	1944-47	1958-61
Assessment*	$ 5679	$ 2640	$ 6560	$ 4815
Tax rate	.01036	.02850	.01216	.03640
Total Tax	58.83	75.24	79.77	175.27
City-parish budget+	18.33	34.25	59.26	58.01
Designated for schools, recreation and court-house #	40.50	40.99	20.51	117.26
Paid by State Property Tax Relief Fund"	7.41	30.71	10.61	44.97

*Rural assessments in 1944-47 included industrial and suburban areas. City assessments in 1958-61 include the expanded city limits to encompass an additional 30 square miles containing another 30,000 taxpayers.

+Computed by dividing budgeted property tax revenues by number of taxpayers.

#Difference between total taxes and amount allocated to the city parish budget.

"Computed by applying the percentage of assessed value covered by homestead exemption to the derived tax load per taxpayer.

Industries located in the industrial area pay the parish-wide taxes on the assessed value of properties not covered by the ten-year industry exemption. In 1958-61, each industry paid an average of $44,654.97 per year. Without the industrial exemption each industry would have paid $88,124.80, or almost twice as much.

Use of Property Taxes

The bulk of property tax revenue is channeled into the school system. About 78 per cent of the parish-wide taxes go to support parish schools. This amounted to an average of $9,648,186 per year during 1958-61, only a million dollars less than the total cost of city-parish government. Another 14 per cent, or $1,715,919, was allocated to parish administration. Six per cent, or $686,367, went to recreation, and 2 per cent, or $203,449, for the courthouse fund, Figure XXVI.

Proportion of Property Taxpayers to Population

It might be argued that cost per capita is not a good measure of cost of local government because the property owners bear the brunt of property taxes, and the number of property owners may not increase in number as population increases. Surprisingly, however, the total number of taxpayers in the parish increased 125 per cent

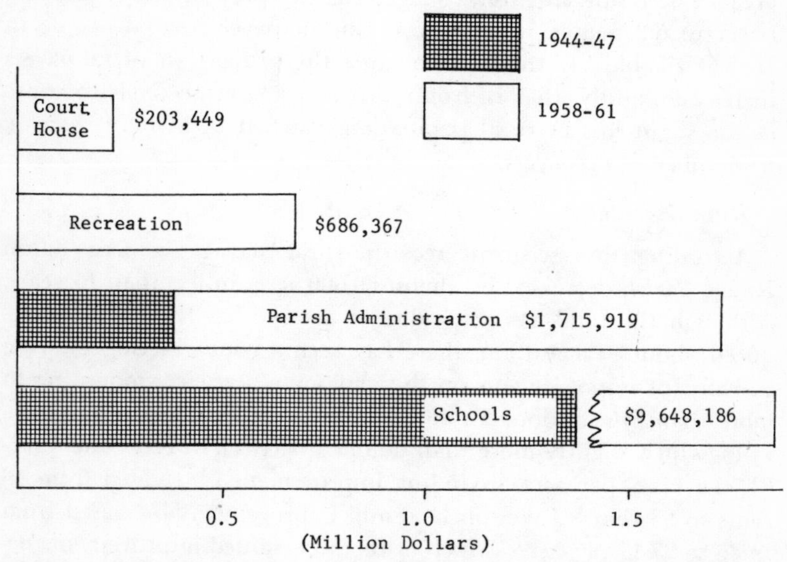

FIGURE XXVI Allocation of Average Revenues from Parish-Wide Property Taxes, East Baton Rouge Parish, 1944-47 and 1958-61

TABLE 21

Population, Number of Taxpayers, and Cost per Taxpayer in Baton Rouge and East Baton Rouge Parish, 1944-47 and 1958-61

	Population		Property Taxpayers	
	1944-47	1958-61	1944-47	1958-61
City	42,832	151,200	6,931	39,795
Rural	72,694	72,570	20,684	22,355
Total	115,526	223,770	27,615	62,150
	People per Taxpayer		Property Tax Per Taxpayer*	
City	6.2	3.8	$79.77	$175.27
Rural	3.5	3.2	58.83	75.24
Total	4.2	3.6	28.60	49.47

*Includes taxes for schools, recreation and courthouse maintenance. See Table 20.

between 1944-47 and 1958-61, while population increased only 94 per cent. Naturally, the city population and number of property taxpayers in the city would be expected to increase, especially in light of the expanded city limits which encircled populous suburban areas. The result, in effect, changed the city proportions of one taxpayer to 6.2 people in 1944-47 to one taxpayer per 3.8 people in 1958-61, Table 21. In the rural area the proportion of taxpayers increased slightly, that is, from 1:3.5 to 1:3.2, respectively, because of the slight loss in rural population matched by a slight increase in number of taxpayers.

Rural Acreage and Taxes

According to assessment records, rural acreage in East Baton Rouge Parish decreased by almost 66,000 acres in less than 15 years. Although the total assessed value of acreage has thereby been reduced about $1.6 million, there has been a counteracting increase in value of improvements on the remaining acreage, amounting to more than $10 million, Table 22. Because of the increased millage rates, which slightly more than doubled between 1944-47 and 1958-61, the taxes per acre, excluding improvements, increased from 43 cents to 93 cents. Taxes on land and improvements increased from $1.86 to $7.17 per acre. (Much of the high valued improvements occurred in the suburban area.) From a 20 per cent sample of rural properties assessed during 1946 and 1960, and by applying an aver-

TABLE 22
Rural Acreage and Taxes, 1944-47 and 1958-61

	Annual Averages	
	1944-47	1958-61
Rural Acreage*	242,534	176,729
Assessed Value of Acreage*	$ 6,411,304.00	$ 4,816,029.00
Assessed Value of Improvements on Country Real Estate*	$21,523,452.00	$ 32,214,769.00
Basic Millage Rate+		
(1) Parish	10.36	28.50
(2) State	5.75	5.75
Taxes on land#	$ 103,286.11	$ 164,949.00
Taxes on improvements#	$ 346,742.81	$ 1,103,355.84
Taxes per Acre "		
(1) Land only	$0.43	$0.93
(2) Land and improvements	$1.86	$7.17
(3) Farmland**	$0.42	$1.31
Assessment Ratio**´	51.7%	9.7%
Market Value of land & improvements++	$54,032,410.00	$381,760,804.00
Taxes per $1,000 Market Value## (Farmland)	$8.33	$3.32

*From reports of Louisiana Tax Commission, includes suburban and timber land. Excludes marshland and miscellaneous land.

+Excluding Special District millage rates as reported by assessor.

#Computed by applying basic millage rate to assessed value.

"Computed by dividing taxes by acreage.

**Computed from 20% sample of farm properties, using average value of $54 per acre in 1945 and $393 in 1960, per Agri. Census reports.

++Assessed value divided by assessment ratio.

##Total property taxes divided by market value.

age value of $54 per acre in 1946 and a value of $393 per acre in 1960, it was determined that the assessment ratio (assessed value to market value) was 51.7 per cent in 1944-47 and 9.7 per cent in 1958-61. Based on these data, it can be said that the market value of farm land and added improvements in 1960 had a value more than seven times greater than in 1945. Furthermore, rural taxes per $1,000 of market value amounted to $8.33 per thousand in 1944-47 as compared to $3.32 per thousand in 1958-61.

Summary of Costs per Capita and per Rural Taxpayer

When comparing per capita costs for 1944-47 with 1958-61, in comparable dollars, the cost of city-parish government showed an increase for every category of expenditures except capital expenditures, and contributions to other agencies. The per capita city-parish cost averaged $18.69 per year in 1944-47 and $47.65 in 1958-61. Particular attention is again directed to the fact that the costs analyzed here include only those reported in the city-parish audits and do not include costs of the local school system and other autonomous state-constituted agencies. (Total property taxes allocated to local government, including schools, recreation, and courthouse maintenance, amounted to $55.00 per capita in the parish during the period 1958-61.)[9] Expenditures for public works and capital improvements accounted for almost two-thirds of local government expenditures, while fire protection and police protection each utilized nearly one-fifth of the total budget. Since consolidation, a parish-wide one per cent sales tax was added as a source of revenue, and in 1958-61 provided one-third of city-parish funds. Thus, expanded services were made possible without placing an added burden on property taxpayers. This undoubtedly contributed to the success of the consolidation. State aid continued to increase but retained about the same relationship to the total, i.e., about 15 per cent of the combined city-parish budgets in 1958-61.

The total number of property taxpayers, including public utilities, more than doubled during the study period, thus reflecting the rate of development of new properties. Likewise, special districts continued to sprout profusely in suburban areas. The average assessed value of farmland, without improvements, remained at $18.00 per acre, both before and after consolidation. The value of improvements, however, increased from $10.00 per acre in 1944-47 to $20.00 in 1958-61. Although individual assessments on land and improvements were fairly stable during the fifteen-year interval, the rise in millage rates succeeded in increasing farm real estate taxes from 42 cents per acre in 1945 to $1.31 in 1960. Assessment ratios changed from about 52 per cent in 1945 to about 10 per cent in 1960, and taxes on farm acreage for these respective periods averaged $8.33 per thousand dollars of market value compared to $3.32. Thus, the rural tax burden, in relation to market value of rural properties, is much more favorable today than it was 15 or 20 years ago. In fact, the rapidly declining assessment ratio can be interpreted to mean that the property tax burden on farm acreage decreased about 60 per cent (from $8.33 to $3.32) in 1945-60.

Chapter VI

Consolidation: A Real Or Deferred Solution?

THE MODIFIED consolidation of the City of Baton Rouge and East Baton Rouge Parish which was inaugurated with the adoption of the *Plan of Government* now has approximately fifteen years of experience behind it. From an organizational standpoint, the plan undoubtedly provided a substantial basis from which to approach the problems of the metropolitan area on a unified basis. Measured by almost any criteria, the pre-1949 delineations of community types within the parish and the general governing bodies responsible for local public services were inadequate. The boundaries of the old city bore no relation to the extent of urbanization, the relation of both city and "rural" areas to the major industrial sites within the parish was undefined, and coordination between the parish and city governing authorities was haphazard to say the least. A geographical entity which was socially and economically interdependent was almost totally lacking in the governmental institutions necessary to effect the public services implied by this interdependence or to play its appropriate role in the creation of a larger measure of community identity among the residents of the metropolitan area. If consolidation did not produce a single government for the entire metropolitan complex, it did create the conditions for coordinating rural, urban, and industrial area government by means of governing councils with overlapping memberships and a single executive. The personalized and fragmented administrative system previously in operation was effectively displaced; and the new government could easily be conceived to be *the* government upon which responsibility could be fixed.

From a standpoint of the orthodox precepts of local government organization some important deficiencies still exist in the Baton Rouge consolidation. In the first place, the metropolitan area continues to be governed by two councils rather than by a unified local authority. Although the councils overlap in membership, the rural area councilmen have shown increasing signs of being restive under a plan which precludes their participation in decisions relating to the incorporated area, decisions which they consider as directly affecting the areas outside the city. As early as 1951, the first study commitee actually approved a motion recommending that "city-parish council members vote on all the issues of both the city and parish, and have a common council for both city and parish." [1] At a later meeting of the committee, however, it was pointed out that Art. VIII, Sec. thirteen of the Louisiana constitution (making ineligible for office persons who are not qualified electors of the state, district, parish, municipality, or ward in which the functions of the office are performed) apparently prevented such a merger.

As indicated in the first chapter, the proposed charter amendment to accomplish the complete merger of the two councils was defeated by the voters in 1952. The action necessary to implement complete consolidation of the two councils has been deliberated in subsequent study committees, but was deferred in each instance. Even if a constitutional amendment permitting the merger were approved, problems concerning the constitutional authority of taxation and eligibility for homestead tax exemption, which were previously indicated, would have to be approached cautiously in order not to jeopardize either existing municipal tax sources or state rebates to the parish in lieu of homestead exemptions. Despite these thorny legal issues, both incumbent rural council members (from Wards Two and Three) strongly express the view that their areas require many more city-type services than can presently be extended to them and both seem to feel that a unified council might make an extension of such services possible on a less costly basis than is now afforded through special districts.[2] However, unless the unified council had the authority to levy both parish and municipal taxes in any part of the parish, and unless corporate municipal powers could be extended to cover any areas needing municipal services (either complete or piecemeal) outside the present incorporated area, it is difficult to see how the problems that they indicate could be effectively solved. A mere merger of the councils, without breaking down existing boundaries within the parish, would not do the job.

Other closely related problems arise from the continuation of a substantial measure of separation between city and parish. Although the city has expanded by annexation since consolidation, this expansion has been slight in terms of the growth of the suburban fringe. The method of annexation provided in the plan has not encouraged the type of municipal expansion or general extension of urban services necessary to keep pace with urban growth. The proliferation of special tax districts for the purpose of providing municipal-type services on a service-by-service basis to urbanized communities in the "rural" area is symptomatic of the difficulty. It may be argued that the street lighting districts, garbage districts, and fire districts in the parish do not present the same type of problem that special districts do in some other governmental jurisdictions. They do not involve, for example, additional governing authorities, administrative overhead, or special work crews and equipment because these are supplied through the existing local governmental institutions. The justification for continued use of this fractionated special district system is that residents have the opportunity to acquire additional public services if they are willing to pay the price. It is not necessary for an entire city to agree on having the service before it can be made available. Even so, it is apparent that the costs to residents of the special districts for these piecemeal services is quite high in comparison with the unified provision of comparable services within the city. The time seems appropriate to consider a further wholesale annexation[3] or a broader extension of the compound-functional consolidation in order to meet service needs on a more systematic basis and halt the proliferation of special districts.

The problem of representation is also a factor of increasing importance. The rural wards, which were slightly over-represented in terms of proportionality of population when consolidation was achieved, are now seriously under-represented. On a strict population basis, Ward Two would already be entitled to a minimum of two councilmen. Attempts at reapportioning the councils undoubtedly will re-open such questions as the single-member district versus at-large memberships and might very well exacerbate some of the old area conflicts and tendencies toward administrative dispersal that experience with the plan has muted. The concentration of administrative responsibility in the office of the mayor-president was one of the outstanding accomplishments of the consolidated plan of government. The establishment of unified executive control over major line functions, budgetary matters, and staff activities has undoubtedly helped to systematize and coordinate the administration of major functions of local government in both parish and city. A personnel merit system has been introduced, an effective central records management program established, and fiscal and accounting responsibilities have been unified. The city-parish government now has a chief executive who is equipped with the authority and tools to plan and manage the administrative affairs assigned to him; in turn this concentration of authority makes it possible for the mayor-president to be held accountable for deficiencies of administration.

These favorable developments are conditioned by the fact that there is still a considerable dispersal of control over some functions of local government. In consequence, there is also duplication, either of function or staff activity, at some points. A large part of this problem results from the compromise necessitated by the entrenchment of the parish constitutional officers. The direct election of a multiplicity of officials, each of whom is separately and directly accountable to the public, certainly violates the standard proverbs of administrative organization, expands administrative overhead, tends toward duplication of functions (as in the case of law enforcement), and increases the difficulty of coordination. Short of a complete revamping of existing local government boundaries and administrative structures, however, it is difficult to visualize a means of dealing with these intransigent factors. It is readily apparent that consolidation did not eliminate all duplication of agencies and services. The city and parish still prepare separate budgets and maintain separate accounts of revenues and expenditures. In effect, most of the city functions that prevailed before consolidation are continued as city functions. Likewise, most of the parish functions retain their former identities.

Much of the financial support for constitutional offices comes from fees and commissions directly related to the services they provide. Nevertheless, the city-parish government contributes office space and considerable financial support to many of the constitutional offices, particularly for care and feeding of prisoners, clerk of court, family court, district attorney, coroner, district court and registrar of voters. One unit of local government that retained its independent status and was not included in the city-parish consolidation was the school board. Its powers and duties are granted by state law and neither the city nor the parish councils have jurisdiction over school board revenues and expenditures. The audit of school board records continues to be a responsibility of the state supervisor of public funds. Other problems of an administrative nature persist, too. As a matter of logic, there does not seem to be any reason for the fire and police civil service system to be administered separately from the general personnel system of the city-parish. By the same token, it is not easy to understand the continued independence of the recreation and parks commission, which is not directly accountable to any elective legislative or executive agency. There are, of course, legal obstacles to the merger of these two functions into the general government, but these apparently could be overcome fairly easily if the urge to continued separation on the part of those most directly involved were not so strong.

In terms of the development of new services and expansion of existing services to meet piled-up needs, the record under consolidation is impressive. The most important new services have been those furnishd by the planning department. Even if it is conceded that a planning program might have been developed under the pre-1949 governmental system, there is no reason to assume that its services would have extended beyond the boundaries of the city, with the result that many of the tangible, and even more of the intangible, benefits of planning (such as the coordinating effects produced by planning the development of facilities on a parish-wide basis) would have been lost. Even with the availability of planning services, the problems of maintaining an orderly basis for the rapid growth that the parish has undergone have taxed the administrative and fiscal resources of the area so heavily that the imagination balks at the thought of what might have occurred without them. It is difficult to determine with any great degree of precision whether local government administration is at a more efficient level as a result of consolidation. Local conditions are not the same as before consolidation. Capital investments made earlier serve as a base for continued growth and development. Public needs have changed, new standards of living have been achieved, and fringe benefits to employees have added considerably to costs.

In appraising the local government services which antedated the consolidation, we have concentrated most of our attention on the department of public works. This course was followed for two reasons: in the first place, this research project was designed primarily to explore the effects of consolidation on the rural sector of the parish, and the department of public works is the department which is responsible for the overwhelming proportion of local government functions in the unincorporated area; secondly, public works is the line department whose organization and operations are most fully consolidated under the plan of government. It should be emphasized at this point that, on balance, the city (including the areas newly incorporated under the plan) derived the most immediate benefits from the consolidated government. Both the municipal fire and police departments have undergone complete renovations, and substantial improvements have been made in traffic circulation, garbage collection, street maintenance and development, and street lighting in the incorporated area.[4] The attention accorded the city during the earliest period of the plan's operation was not simply a matter of the city's having made a better bargain in moving toward consolidation than the rural areas; the city was the area of most urgent need insofar as public services were concerned, and five-sixths of the new city consisted of sectors of the parish previously under a rural-type government. Even before the most crucial needs of the city were met, however, programs were underway to improve rural area roads and drainage. And while these projects have been somewhat limited by conditions described in the chapter on public works, the volume and quality of service in these fields of primary interest to the rural residents completely outstrip the efforts prior to 1949. But even if the measurable differences in service levels are left aside, there is an impressive record, under consolidation, of preparation of the rural area for the increasing urbanization that it has undergone and is undergoing. Strict lines of separation once marked out local boundaries within the parish, but these have largely been swept away in the interest of unifying the whole community physically; and the physical unification has led to a stronger sense of local identity in terms of the larger dimension. Accessibility by road from any part of the parish to any other part has been greatly facilitated, and the mere presence on road and drainage works of *city-parish* crews in *city-parish* vehicles is sufficient to call attention to the interdependence of the entire metropolitan community The extension of planning and subdivision regulation to the entire parish was another government activity which had the dual effect of preparing for sound future growth and bringing the entire parish into closer unity. Finally, the consolidation of the sanitary sewer system and the expansion of its facilities beyond the limits of the heavily built-up areas and into the areas of greatest potential growth is a significant physical symbol of the civic maturation of an urbanized area that retains some rural components.

Neither the scope nor the resources of this research project on city-parish consolidation permitted a survey of the attitudes of local residents toward the plan of government. Such a survey should be well worth the effort from the standpoint of the knowledge it might yield about the responses of citizens to the change and their perceptions of existing service standards and deficiencies. Even in the absence of such a survey, it is possible to conjecture that the plan works to the reasonable satisfaction of most of the area's residents, including those in the sections from which most of the original opposition came. There is no reason to suppose that this is a mere matter of passive adjustment to an innovation that was originally resisted. On the contrary, the obvious physical changes that have taken place under the plan seem to have produced a favorable public reaction, and a considerable amount of retrospective pride is evidenced among many sectors of the community in the uniqueness of the plan and its successful installation in the face of considerable odds. Each of the last two committees established to review the system has expressed strong confidence in the plan; and despite discontent on the part of the rural members of the parish council with some of its details, neither of them would want to abandon the consolidated plan. As the councilman who has served for more than eleven years from Ward Two has said, "the prime factor to keep in mind is that under this plan even today more money is being spent in the rural areas than ever would have been under the old system. The Police Jury system ... just won't work in a highly industrialized parish such as ours."[5] Several rural taxpayers have also stated that the consolidation has resulted in effective coordination of public works in rural areas. For example, ward boundaries formerly marked the abrupt halt of road construction or road maintenance. Now the work is planned and carried out on a parish-wide basis, without segmented control by smaller political subdivisions.

As an object lesson in an approach to the metropolitan area problem in communities which combine urban sprawl with substantial surrounding rural sectors, the Baton Rouge consolidation is as valuable for its demonstration of the limits on what is possible in local government change as it is for the display of the more positive effects of the experiment. No matter how urgent the need for change may appear to those closest to the local government scene, and however logical the recommended solution may be, it is important not to discount the inertia produced by the innate political conservatism of an existing community. This natural tendency to cling to known and established government, even when its utility lags in the face of social change, provides a cautionary note which is strongly underlined by the Baton Rouge experience. Only the most careful advance planning, followed by an intensive public relations campaign, enabled the plan to succeed, and even then a considerable amount of sheer good luck was involved. The proponents of the plan were able to take advantage of some highly favorable conditions in the particular situation facing them. The state constitution could be amended fairly easily to accommodate the type of change desired and to permit a referendum that was less constrictive than usual; the metropolitan area was contained within the boundaries of a single parish; and there were only two small municipal corporations other than Baton Rouge in the area. Those primarily responsible for the charter's development were also willing to compromise in order not to jeopardize the possibility of some change. They did not attempt to buck insuperable odds by abolishing all vestiges of existing institutions (e.g., the parish constitutional offices), and they moderated their proposals to take account of popular antipathies in cases such as the council-manager form of government.

In the final analysis, the groups which provided the initiative for the plan did not cease their efforts once final popular and legal approvals had been attained. At the lowest points in its struggle for survival, the plans had the concerted backing of a substantial portion of influential citizens who were determined to see that it was made to work because they regarded it as the last best hope for a solution to the particular metropolitan area problems facing the city and parish. In this connection the creation of the first plan of government review committee proved to be an unexpectedly effective development. The review committee was highly regarded because it was not partisan; and its full public discussion of the strengths and weaknesses of the plan, together with possible alternatives to it, improved public understanding while acting as a sounding board for popular complaints. Furthermore, the proposed amendments which ultimately came out of the committee's actions (albeit in a watered-down version) were evidence of flexibility on the part of the new government in adjusting to the exigencies of a fluid political situation. In establishing the first review committee and in following it up with additional ones at intermittent stages, the city-parish councils opened the way for a noticeable upsurge of interest in local public affairs; every major issue in recent years has been the subject of public hearings and debate based on widespread participation and publicity.

In summary, it may be said that the Baton Rouge consolidation may, if proper restraints are applied, furnish an example for similarly situated communities throughout the country. It will do so, however, not so much in terms of the specifics of the case as in the generalities. The foremost characteristics of the reform, if it may be termed that, is its pragmatism. The Baton Rouge experiment has to be regarded as a success because the city and parish were finally consolidated whereas the history of such attempts is mainly a record of failures. What is more, the system has survived and demonstrates some capacity for the self-correction of weaknesses and possible adaptability to further consolidation. If the success is tempered by certain limitations, it is no more than may be expected, and it is unquestionably a major improvement over the condition of governmental paralysis that seems to afflict so many of the nation's areas of prodigious growth.

Appendix

TABLE 23

Items of Expenditure Included under Departmental Headings, City of Baton Rouge

	1944-47		1958-61	
Legislative & Executive	Commissioners & Mayor	$10,001.07	City Council	$11,305.10
			Mayor-President	3,891.60
			Total	$15,196.70
Judicial	City Court & City Clerk	$9,562.18	City Court	$54,691.11
Administration	Dept. of Finance	$21,046.30	Dept. of Finance	$53,307.74
	Office Expense	3,688.18	Treasurer	84,680.17
	Assessment Rolls	2,378.14	Special Audit	3,750.00
	C.P.A.	2,527.43	Tax Collection	3,924.18
	City Physician	1,187.50	C.P.A.	5,000.00
	Printing & Advert.	1,853.00	City Physician	4,425.00
	Travel	121.10	Records & Reports	11,207.76
	Election Expense	754.71	Public Adm. Service	1,100.00
	Miscellaneous	1,868.62	Interest on Loans	2,180.76
			PBX & Postage	13,637.42
			Election Expenses	1,738.86
			Miscellaneous	5,057.66
	Total	$35,424.98	Total	$190,009.55
Employee Benefits			Retirement	$75,323.80
			Social Security	48,084.28
			Insurance	108,537.20
			Special Benefits	2,098.62
			Athletic Fund	387.44
			Total	$234,431.34
Fire Protection	Fire Department	$126,944.83	Fire Department	$1,327,735.37
	Pension Fund	8,217.35	Pension Fund	141,927.08
	Water Supply (Hydrant Rental)	21,012.33	Water Supply (Hydrant Rental)	118,832,58
	Total	$156,174.51	Total	$1,588,495.03

TABLE 23 *Continued*

	1944-47		1958-61	
Police Protection	Police Department	$110,748.46	Police Department	$1,444,211.82
	Pension Fund	10,452.39	Pension Fund	132,977.27
	Total	$121,200.85	Total	$1,577,189.09
City Constable			City Constable	25,912.86
General Services	Health	$11,250.00	Health	132,109.30
	Library	1,414.52	Library	145,721.10
	Traffic Control & Engineering	750.00	Traffic Control & Engineering	174,500.82
	Recreation	3,125.00	Recreation	1,250.00
			Planning Commission	32,639.88
	Total	$16,539.52	Total	$486,221.10
Dept. of Public Works	Dept. of Public Parks & Streets (Salaries)	$25,969.81	Administration	$46,825.27
	Drainage & Pump Maintenance	10,161.56	Bridge & Canal Maintenance	252,754.28
	Park & Cemetery Maintenance	24,976.90	Central Stores	9,896.80
	Insurance & Bonds	8,324.47	Central Garage	94,525.03
	Public Building Maintenance	7,525.36	Inspection	107,019.50
	Street & Right-of-Way Maintenance	27,868.66	Sewer Mtce.	435,962.09
	Street Lighting	18,103.11	Insurance & Bonds	16,878.87
	Refuse Collection	103,605.35	Public Bldg. Maintenance	73,738.92
	Sundry	7,096.52	Street & Right-of-Way Mtce.	99,566.50
			Street Lighting	208,813.40
			Refuse Collection	792,062.62
			Sundry	4,008.39
	Total	$233,631.74	Total	$2,142,051.67
Capital Expenditures	Dept. of Public Works	$437,644.41	Dept. of Public Works	$427,893.00
	Other	23,143.37	Other	341,816.46
	Total	$460,787.78	Total	$769,709.46

TABLE 23 *Continued*

	1944-47		1958-61	
Contributions to Constitutional Offices	Coroner	753.00	Coroner	$12,736.25
	Sheriff: Feeding & Care of Prisoners	602.88	Sheriff: Feeding & Care of Prisoners	75,650.00
			Assessor	13,469.81
			Family Court	47,660.76
	Total	$1,355.88	Total	$149,516.82
Contributions to Other Agencies	Abbatoir	$37,124.14	Veterans Service Officers	$7,885.00
	Municipal Docks & River Terminals	12,263.14	Safety Council	1,875.00
	S.P.C.A.	1,500.00	Municipal Association	1,867.67
	Others	5,422.38	S.P.C.A.	12,500.00
			Others	17,178.03
			Public Transportation Comm.	2,700.00
			Civil Defense	12,490.00
			National Guard	812.50
			Conference of Mayors	100.00
	Total	$56,309.66	Total	$57,408.20
	Grand Total	$1,100,988.17	Grand Total	$7,290,832.93

TABLE 24

Items of Expenditure included under Departmental Headings, Parish of East Baton Rouge

	1944-47		1958-61	
Legislative & Executive	Police Jury	6,164.46	Mayor-President	$38,760.83
			Parish Council	8,344.27
			Total	$47,105.10
Judicial	City Court	5,400.00	Parish Attorney	$49,460.96
	Court Attendance	5,347.50	Court Costs	180.38
	Jurors & Witnesses	4,126.44		
	Juvenile Court	2,434.10		
	Law Library	440.48		
	Total	$17,748.52		$49,641.34
Administration	Police Juror Sec. & Treas.	$9,694.38	Dept. of Finance	$53,241.90
	Office Sup. & Expenses	1,095.52	Treasurer	36,292.01
	Printing & Advertising	4,161.04	Parish Clerk	44,062.43
	Travel	431.72	Personnel Dept.	27,439.06
	Election Expense	8,481.16	Purchasing Div.	28,744.20
	Sundry	287.91	C.P.A.	4,875.00
			5-Mill Tax Administration	10,802.37
			PBX & Postage	10,529.20
			Salary Adjustment & Contingent Reserve	5,037.90
			Publication of Annual Report	3,027.70
			Rents to Trailways	2,643.75
			Public Adm. Service	1,650.00
			Sundry	12,051.89
	Total	$24,151.73	Total	$240,397.41
Employee Benefits			Retirement	$54,253.47
			Social Security	44,585.31
			Insurance-Employees	46,424.50
			Employees Special Benefits	1,844.54
			Employees Athletic Fund	132.03
			Total	$147,239.85

TABLE 24 *Continued*

	1944-47		1958-61	
Capital Expenditures			Dept. of Public Works	$428,162.23
			Other	209,022.86
	Total for Dept. of Public Wks. & Others	$244,421.77	Total	$637,185.09
Contributions to Constitutional Offices	Sheriff - Feeding Prisoners & Jail Expense	$31,157.24	Sheriff - Feeding Prisoners & Jail Expense	$103,591.26
	Sheriff's Commission	29,667.75	Sheriff's Commission	81,899.40
	Assessor	32,105.31	Assessor	12,607.37
	Clerk of Court	4,653.29	Clerk of Court	146,033.31
	Dist. Attorney	18,762.17	Dist. Attorney	89,589.62
	Coroner	7,532.72	Coroner	38,637.50
	Dist. Court	10,326.04	Dist. Court	42,405.78
	Registrar of Voters	3,261.61	Registrar of Voters	19,562.27
	Justice of the Peace & Constables	3,318.91	Justice of the Peace & Constables	6,435.49
			Family Court	80,061.60
	Total	$140,785.24	Total	$620,823.60
Contributions to Other Agencies	Farm Agent	$4,093.27	Farm Agent	$11,721.50
	American Legion Service Officer	3,400.00	American Legion Service Officer	3,022.52
	Beneficiary Students	2,446.25	Farm Bureau	900.00
	S.P.C.A.	4,250.00	Safety Council	1,875.00
	Planning Survey	2,595.78	National Guard	812.50
	Police Juror Association	316.25	Police Juror Association	1,241.03
	South Louisiana Fair Association	250.00	South Louisiana Fair Association	750.00
	Others	7,032.20	Airport Commission	3,913.50
			Others	16,176.30
	Total	$24,383.75	Total	$40,412.40
Transfer of Funds			Three Mills of Industrial Area Tax to City of Baton Rouge, Baker & Zachary	
	Grand Total	$1,055,885.99	Grand Total	$3,365,662.84

TABLE 24 *Continued*

	1944-47		1958-61	
Fire Protection	Paid to City	$21,780.00		
	Fire Districts #1, #2, #3	27,293.24		
	Fire Hydrant Rental	15,138.54		
	Paid to Zachary Fire Dept.	750.00		
	Equipment	4,895.78		
	Total	$69,857.56		
Police Protection	----		----	
General Services	Traffic Bureau	$1,000.00		
	Health	16,117.92	Health	$50,327.35
	Library	28,500.00	Library	105,616.57
	Recreation Commission	13,250.00	Recreation Commission	250.00
	License Inspection	2,442.58	Planning Commission	21,008.85
	Total	$61,310.50	Total	$177,202.77
Dept. of Public Works	(Were not itemized in early audits)		Administration	$60,350.78
			Bridge & Canal Maintenance	180,778.49
			Central Stores	4,508.54
			Central Garage	43,929.46
			Engineering	178,020.55
			Inspection	97,103.93
			Insurance & Bonds	8,590.70
			Public Bldg. Maintenance	73,317.49
			Sewer Maintenance	108,393.84
			Street Maintenance (Urban)	328,708.91
			Street Maintenance (Rural)	321,952.59
	Total	$467,062.46	Total	$1,405,655.28

Table 25
Annual Expenditure for the City and Parish Combined, East Baton Rouge Parish

	1944-47	1958-61	Adjusted to 1944-47 Purchasing Power
Legislative & Executive	$16,165.53	$62,301.80	$40,496.17
Judicial	27,310.70	104,332.45	67,816.09
Administration	59,576.71	430,406.96	279,764.52
Employee Benefits		381,671.19	248,086.27
Fire Protection	226,032.07	1,588,495.03	1,032,521.77
Police Protection	121,200.85	1,577,189.09	1,025,172.91
City Constable		25,912.86	16,843.36
General Services (Total)	77,850.00	663,423.87	431,225.50
Health	27,367.92	182,436.65	118,583.82
Planning Commission		53,648.73	34,871.67
Traffic Control & Engineering	1,750.00	174,500.82	113,425.53
License Inspection	2,442.58		
Library	29,914.52	251,337.67	163,369.48
Recreation	16,375.00	1,500.00	975.00
Department of Public Works (Total)	700,694.20	3,547,706.95	2,306,009.52
Administration		107,176.05	69,664.43
Bridge & Canal Maintenance	*	433,532.77	281,796.30
Central Stores		14,405.34	9,363.47
Central Garage		138,454.49	89,995.42
Inspection		204,123.43	132,680.23
Engineering		178,020.55	115,713.36
Insurance & Bonds		25,469.57	16,555.22
Public Bldg. Maint.		147,056.41	95,586.67
Sewer Maintenance		544,355.93	353,831.35
Streets & Right-of-Way Maint.		750,228.00	487,648.20

TABLE 25 *Continued*

	1944-47	1958-61	Adjusted to 1944-47 Purchasing Power
Drainage & Pump Maint.			
Park & Cemetery Maint.			
Street Lighting		$208,813.40	$135,728.71
Refuse Collection		792,062.62	514,840.70
Sundry		4,008.39	2,605.45
Capital Expenditures	$705,209.55	1,406,894.55	914,484.71
Contributions to Constitutional Offices	142,141.12	770,340.42	500,721.27
Sheriff - Feeding & Transporting Prisoners	31,760.12	179,241.26	116,506.82
Sheriff's Commission	29,667.95	81,899.40	53,234.61
Assessor	32,105.31	26,077.18	16,950.17
Clerk of Court	4,653.29	146,033.31	94,921.65
District Attorney	18,762.17	89,589.62	58,233.25
District Court	10,326.04	42,405.78	27,563.76
Coroner	8,285.72	51,373.75	33,392.94
Registrar of Voters	3,261.61	19,562.27	12,715.48
Family Court		127;722.36	83,019.53
Justices of the Peace & Constables	3,318.91	6,435.49	4,183.07
Contributions to Other Agencies	80,693.41	97,820.60	63,583.39
Transfer of three-mill Industrial Tax to Baker, Zachary, and Baton Rouge			
	$2,156,874.16	$10,656,495.77	$6,926,722.25

*No breakdown available.

TABLE 26

Cost of Government Services, per Capita, City of Baton Rouge, 1944-47 and 1958-61

	Cost per Capita		
	1944-47	1958-61	Adjusted*
Executive & Legislative	.23	.10	.07
Judicial	.22	.36	.24
Administration	.83	1.26	.82
Employee Benefits	-	1.55	1.00
Fire Protection	3.65	10.51	6.83
Police Protection	2.83	10.43	6.78
Feeding & Care of Prisoners	.02	.50	.33
City Constable	-	.17	.11
General Services			
Health	.26	.87	.57
Planning Commission	-	.21	.14
Library	.03	.96	.63
Traffic Control & Engineering	.02	1.15	.75
Recreation	.07	.01	-
Dept. of Public Works (Total)	5.45	14.18	9.21
Administration	-	.31	.20
Bridge & Canal Maintenance	-	1.67	1.09
Central Stores	-	.07	.04
Central Garage	-	.63	.41
Inspection		.71	.46
Insurance & Bonds	.19	.11	.07
Public Bldg. Maintenance	.18	.49	.32

TABLE 26 *Continued*

	Cost per Capita 1944-47	1958-61	Adjusted*
Sewer Maintenance	-	2.88	1.87
Street & Right-of-Way Maintenance	.65	.66	.43
Street Lighting	.42	1.38	.90
Refuse Collection	2.42	5.24	3.40
Drainage & Pump Maintenance	.24	-	-
Park & Cemetery Maintenance	.58	-	-
Sundry	.17	.03	.02
Capital Expenditures			
D.P.W.	10.22	2.83	1.84
Other	.54	2.26	1.47
Contributions to Constitutional Offices			
Assessor	-	.09	.06
Coroner	.02	.08	.05
Family Court	-	.32	.20
Contributions to Other Agencies	1.31	.38	.25
	25.69	48.21	31.34

*1958-61 values adjusted to 1944-47 purchasing power.

TABLE 27

Cost of Government Services, per Capita, City of Baton Rouge, 1944-47 and 1958-61

	Cost per Capita		
	1944-47	1958-61	Adjusted*
Executive & Legislative	.08	.65	.42
Judicial	.24	.68	.44
Administration	.33	3.31	2.15
Employee Benefits		2.03	1.32
Fire Protection	.96	-	-
Feeding & Transporting Prisoners	.43	1.43	.93
General Services			
Traffic Bureau	.01	-	-
Health	.22	.69	.45
Library	.39	1.45	.94
Recreation	.18	-	-
License Inspection	.03	-	-
Planning Commission	-	.29	.19
Dept. of Public Works (Total)	6.42	19.36	12.59
Administration	-	.83	.54
Bridge & Canal Maintenance	-	2.49	1.62
Central Stores	-	.06	.04
Central Garage	-	.61	.40
Engineering	-	2.45	1.59
Inspection	-	1.34	.87
Insurance & Bonds	-	.12	.08
Public Bldg. Maintenance	.50	1.01	.66
Sewer Maintenance	.03	1.49	.97
Street Maintenance	-	8.96	5.82
Drainage	.08	-	-

TABLE 27 *Continued*

	Cost per Capita		
	1944-47	1958-61	Adjusted*
Capital Expenditures	3.36	8.78	5.71
Contribution to Constitutional Offices			
Sheriff's Commission	.41	1.13	.73
Assessor	.44	.17	.11
Clerk of Court	.06	2.01	1.31
District Attorney	.26	1.23	.80
Coroner	.10	.53	.34
District Court	.14	.58	.38
Registrar of Voters	.04	.27	.18
Justices of the Peace & Constable	.04	.09	.06
Family Court	-	1.11	.72
Contributions to Other Agencies	.34	.56	.36
Transfer of three-mill Industrial Tax to City of Baker, Zachary, & Baton Rouge			
	14.48	46.35	30.13

*1958-61 values adjusted to 1944-47 purchasing power.

TABLE 28
Cost of Government Services, per Capita, City of Baton Rouge and East Baton Rouge Parish Combined, 1944-47 and 1958-61

	Cost per Capita		
	1944-47	1958-61	Adjusted*
Legislative & Executive	.14	.28	.18
Judicial	.24	.47	.31
Administration	.52	1.92	1.25
Employee Benefits	-	1.71	1.11
Fire Protection	1.96	7.10	4.62
Police Protection	1.05	7.05	4.58
Feeding & Transporting Prisoners	.27	.80	.52
City Constable	-	.12	.08
General Services			
Health	.24	.82	.53
Planning Commission	-	.24	.16
Traffic Control & Engineering	.02	.78	.51
License Inspection	.02	-	-
Library	.26	1.12	.73
Recreation	.14	.01	.01
Dept. of Public Works (Total)	6.07	15.85	10.29
Administration	-	.48	.31
Bridge & Canal Maintenance	-	1.94	1.26
Central Stores	-	.06	.04
Central Garage	-	.62	.40
Engineering	-	.80	.52
Inspection	-	.91	.59
Insurance & Bonds	-	.11	.07

TABLE 28 *Continued*

	Cost per Capita		
	1944-47	1958-61	Adjusted*
Public Bldg. Maintenance	-	.66	.43
Refuse Collection	-	3.54	2.30
Sewer Maintenance	-	2.43	1.58
Street & Right-of-Way Maintenance	-	3.35	2.18
Street Lighting	-	.93	.60
Sundry	-	.02	.01
Capital Expenditures	6.10	6.29	4.09
Contributions to Constitutional Offices (Total)	.96	2.65	1.72
Sheriff's Commission	.26	.37	.24
Assessor	.28	.12	.08
Clerk of Court	.04	.65	.42
District Attorney	.16	.40	.26
Coroner	.07	.23	.15
District Court	.09	.19	.12
Registrar of Voters	.03	.09	.06
Justices of the Peace & Constables	.03	.03	.02
Family Court	-	.57	.37
Contributions to Other Agencies	.70	.44	.29
Transfer of three-Mill Industrial Tax to City of Baker, Zachary, & Baton Rouge			
	18.69	47.65	30.97

*1958-61 values adjusted to 1944-47 purchasing power.

TABLE 29

Sources of Revenue, General Fund, City of Baton Rouge, 1944-47 and 1958-61

	1944-47		1958-61	
	Annual Average	Per cent of Total	Annual Average	Per cent of Total
Property Taxes	$326,183.40	49.12	$2,054,364.96	28.0
Sales Tax	-	-	2,644,219.29	36.0
Excise Taxes*	32,876.98	4.95	328,866.79	4.5
Licenses & Permits	193,672.29	29.17	961,712.33	13.1
Rents, Concessions, & Commissions	58,243.78	8.77	11,105.82	.2
Fines, Forfeits, & Fees	30,615.90	4.61	286,223.40	3.9
State Aid	12,878.56	1.94	899,387.41	12.2
Miscellaneous	9,561.72	1.44	67,814.51	.9
Unbudgeted Revenues	-		94,812.10	1.3
Total	$664,032.63	100.00	$7,348,506.61	100.1

*For use of streets by public conveyances and public utilities.

TABLE 30

Sources of Revenue, General Fund, City of Baton Rouge, 1944-47 and 1958-61

	1944-47		1958-61	
	Annual Average	Per cent of Total	Annual Average	Per cent of Total
Property Taxes	$463,691.03	44.83	$1,710,510.56	42.5
Sales Tax			893,237.42	22.2
Licenses & Permits	121,467.86	11.74	207,059.69	5.2
State Aid	238,332.73	23.04	860,950.90	21.4
Fines, Forfeits, & Fees	10,486.19	1.03	60,289.01	1.5
Contributions from Other Agencies and Funds*	188,092.84	18.18	215,978.00	5.4
Miscellaneous	12,221.77	1.18	11,292.28	.3
Unbudgeted Revenues			59,692.50	1.5
Total	$1,034,292.42	100.00	$4,019,010.44	100.0

*Also includes refunds from other funds, and bank loans.

TABLE 31

Sources of Revenue, General Fund, City and Parish Combined, Baton Rouge, 1944-47 and 1958-61

	1944-47		1958-61	
	Annual Average	Per cent of Total	Annual Average	Per cent of Total
Property Taxes	$789,874.43	46.5	$3,764,875.52	33.1
Sales Tax			3,537,456.71	31.1
Excise Taxes	32,876.98	1.9	328,866.79	2.9
Licenses & Permits	315,140.15	18.6	1,168,772.02	10.3
Rents, Concessions & Commissions	58,243.78	3.4	11,105.82	.1
Fines, Forfeits, & Fees	41,102.09	2.4	346,512.41	3.0
State Aid	251,211.29	14.8	1,760,338.39	15.5
Contributions from Other Agencies & Funds	188,092.84	11.1	215,978.00	1.9
Miscellaneous	21,783.49	1.3	79,106.79	.7
Unbudgeted Revenues			154,504.60	1.4
Total	$1,698,325.05	100.0	$11,367,517.05	100.0

TABLE 32

Tax Revenues Other than Property Taxes and Sales Taxes, Parish and City, 1944-47 and 1958-61

Year	Severance Tax to the Parish	Gasoline Tax to the Parish	Tobacco Tax to the City	Special Grants to Parish+	Beer Tax Parish	Beer Tax City	Chain Store Tax Parish	Chain Store Tax Cit
1944	$20,844.24	$185,303.23	-	-	-	-	$4,790.27	-
1945	13,572.37	198,158.54	-	-	-	-	4,911.95	-
1946	9,863.08	239,648.70	-	-	-	-	4,921.12	-
1947	10,314.98	260,305.85	-	-	-	$38,435.97	696.60	$13,078
Average 1944-47	$13,648.67	$220,854.08	-	-	-	-	3,829.98	-
1958	$11,717.58	$648,663.60	$692,457.41	$95,980.92	$20,165.25	$102,391.41	$3,145.09	$12,122
1959	13,896.53	734,307.21	773,254.84	96,343.44	20,398.47	103,110.27	2,633.73	12,779
1960	9,846.24	745,943.00	812,513.71	96,718.12	24,177.74	104,506.53	6,052.02	13,880
1961	10,230.52	774,510.37	808,874.53	95,584.82	25,718.44	102,930.83	7,770.53	17,821
Average 1958-61	$11,422.72	$725,856.04	$771,775.12	$96,156.82	$22,614.98	$103,234.76	$4,900.34	$14,150

*These special tax revenues are included as state aid in Tables 29, 30, and 31.

+Includes grants for street maintenance as part of continuation of state highways, and for purchase of gravel.

Table 33

Total Contributions to Constitutional Offices by City and Parish Government, East Baton Rouge Parish

	1944-47	1958-61	Adjusted to 1944-47 Purchasing Power
Sheriff	$61,428.07	$261,140.66	$169,741.43
Clerk of Court	4,653.29	146,033.31	94,921.65
Family Court		127,722.36	83,019.53
District Attorney	18,762.17	89,589.62	58,233.25
Coroner	8,285.72	51,373.75	33,392.94
District Court	10,326.04	42,405.78	27,563.76
Assessor	32,105.31	26,077.18	16,950.17
Registrar of Voters	3,261.61	19,562.27	12,715.48
Justices of the Peace and Constables	3,318.91	6,435.49	4,183.07
Total	$142,141.12	$770,340.42	$500,721.28

Table 34

evenues and Expenditures for Garbage, Road Lighting, and Scotlandville Fire Protection Districts, East Baton Rouge Parish, 1958-61

	Garbage Districts		Road Lighting Districts		Scotlandville Fire Protection District	
	Revenues	Expenditures	Revenues	Expenditures	Revenues	Expenditures
	$42,661.60	$32,551.05	$22,450.42	$15,915.63	$37,006.72	$36,937.18
	58,178.71	47,749.69	56,927.49	23,589.78	42,852.29	40,124.87
	66,771.21	53,439.57	53,171.77	51,859.15	50,528.51	43,115.04
	70,501.97	57,855.28	123,162.76	93,873.34	53,354.13	42,913.11
ge 61	$59,528.37	$47,898.90	$63,928.11	$46,309.48	$45,935.41	$40,772.55

Table 35
Assessed Value of Property in City, Rural, and Industrial Areas of East Baton Rouge Parish, 1944-47 and 1958-61

	Assessed Values			
Year	Parish	Rural	City	Industrial
1944	$153,907,041	$109,937,026	$43,970,015	
1945	157,301,485	111,517,138	45,784,347	*
1946	163,781,825	116,404,068	47,377,757	
1947	179,208,724	128,418,305	50,790,419	
Average 1944-47	$163,549,768	$116,569,134	$46,980,634	
1958	394,668,640	49,176,198	179,285,235	$166,207,207
1959	426,417,880	53,968,270	188,738,045	183,711,565
1960	441,622,650	64,039,175	196,156,865	181,426,610
1961	453,209,940	69,885,835	202,669,275	180,654,830
Average 1958-61	$428,979,778	$59,267,370	$191,712,355	$178,000,053

*Industrial area not differentiated 1944-47.

Notes

Chapter II

1 The most comprehensive description of the entire movement for consolidation is Donald George Rhodes, "The Baton Rouge City-Parish Consolidation: A History and Evaluation" (unpublished M.A. thesis, Louisiana State University, 1956). The following description relies heavily on the valuable and detailed research presented in Rhodes's thesis. Other pertinent sources of a general nature include: Jimmy M. Stoker, *Our City-Parish Government: A Thumbnail Sketch* (Baton Rouge: Junior Chamber of Commerce, 1954); C. G. Whitwell, "The New Parish City Government of Baton Rouge," *Southwest Social Science Quarterly* (Dec., 1948); and R. Gordon Kean, Jr., "Consolidation that Works," *National Municipal Review*, Vol. XLV, No. 10 (Nov., 1956), 478-85, 493.

2 John F. Willmott, "City-County Consolidation," *Notes and References*, Vol. IV (New York: Governmental Research Association, 1948).

3 Most of the general description of parish government outlined here draws upon William C. Havard, *The Government of Louisiana* (Louisiana State University: Bureau of Public Administration, 1958), chap. x. See also the chapter by Emmett Asseff on Louisiana in *County Government Across the Nation*, ed. Paul W. Wager (Chapel Hill: University of North Carolina Press, 1950).

4 A full discussion of the organization and powers of the parish police juries and of parish government in general is contained in Ida Louise Cooper, "The Police Jury of Louisiana" (unpublished M.A. thesis, Louisiana State University, 1959). Although the governing authority of the parish may exercise only specifically delegated authority and does not have a general grant of "police power," the cumulative

effect of the specifically delegated powers is extensive and embraces a sizeable number of regulatory and service activities that are normally associated with police powers.

5 One of the most important administrative positions within the appointive power of the police jury or other parish governing body (except in Orleans Parish) is the parish registrar of voters. However, the registrar of voters holds office during good behavior, except that he may be removed at will by the state board of registration, composed of the governor, the lieutenant governor, and the speaker of the state house of representatives. The Orleans registrar is appointed by the governor with the advice and consent of the senate. This is fairly typical of the somewhat loose interplay between state and local powers and responsibilities in relation to the administrative functions performed at the parish level. Both the degrees of centralization and the lines of authority are often difficult to determine; although the registrar of voters may generally be assumed to be a local administrator of state registration laws, the fact remains that in sixty-three of the sixty-four parishes the office is filled by local appointment.

6 The map shows only those districts in which the assessors' rolls indicate the assessment of ad valorem taxes for the indicated purposes. However, the 1947 parish budget implies the existence of at least two additional fire protection districts, as well as some other fire departments in the parish outside the city boundaries. Cited in Rhodes, "The Baton Rouge City-Parish Consolidation," 78.

7 Louisiana holds two general elections: congressional general elections occur every two years on the Tuesday after the first Monday in November (the date that has been made uniform throughout the country by act of congress for the election of national officials); state general elections are preceded by primaries, which, because of one-party domination, usually assume more importance in the eyes of the voters than the general elections.

8 As early as 1941 the health units of the City of Baton Rouge and the Parish of East Baton Rouge had been merged into a single department pursuant to the permissive authority in *Acts of the Legislature, State of Louisiana*, Act 79 (Extraordinary Session, 1921); hereinafter cited *Acts of the Legislature*.

9 Justice of the peace wards do not necessarily follow the same boundaries as the police jury wards.

10 *Constitution, State of Louisiana*, Art. XIV, sec. 3 (b); hereinafter cited *Constitution*.

11 *Acts of the Legislature*, Act 246 (1946).

12 In Louisiana property tax elections, both a majority in numbers of the taxpayers who vote in the election and a majority of the assessed value of the property owned by those voting are required to carry a bond or tax issue.

13 Harland Bartholomew and Associates, *The Master City-Parish Plan, Metropolitan Baton Rouge, Louisiana* (n.p., 1948).

14 *Ibid.*, 1.

15 *Constitution*. Art. XIV, sec. 3(a) (proposed by *Acts of the Legislature*, Act 389 [1946]. Constitutional amendments are an integral part of Louisiana government, over 400 having been adopted since the present constitution was drafted in 1921. Amendments affecting local matters frequently constitute half or more of the proposals before the people at a given election. An amendment is proposed by a two-thirds vote of the members of each house of the state legislature and ratified upon receipt of a popular majority of those voting on the amendment. The voters throughout the state seemingly will approve many local amendments as a matter of course on the assumption that this is the only way to procure changes desired by the residents of the affected locality. Statewide voting on amendments of purely local effect is often very light; the amendment under consideration was approved by a statewide vote of 69,894 to 18,886 with the voters of East Baton Rouge Parish favoring it by 2,987 to 785 votes.

16 "Baton Rouge City-County Plan Submitted," *National Municipal Review*, Vol. XXXVI, No. 7 (July, 1947), 413. Cited in Rhodes, "The Baton Rouge City-Parish Consolidation," 94.

17 *Ibid.*

18 *Morning Advocate* (Baton Rouge), June 13, 1947; *State Times* (Baton Rouge), June 13, 1947, July 9, 1947. Cited in Rhodes, "The Baton Rouge City-Parish Consolidation," 104.

19 Fire and police department employees come under a state fire and police civil service plan which was instituted in 1940 as part of a general reform program put into effect following the 1939 political scandals in Louisiana. This system was made mandatory for all cities with populations between 13,000 and 250,000, and remains in effect to the present. Although examinations are conducted by the state fire and police examiner, participating cities appoint separate municipal fire and police civil service boards for appeal and advisory purposes. (See *Louisana Revised Statutes* of 1950, 33:2471 et seq.); hereinafter cited *La. Rev. Statutes*. New Orleans (over 250,000) is the only large city in the state that includes firemen and policemen in its comprehensive merit system.

20 The parishes collect only two mills of the general parish tax within cities which maintain their own streets, as Baton Rouge did before consolidation. By collecting the entire four mills within the city and undertaking street maintenance there, the parish could obtain state funds in lieu of homestead taxes on the additional two mills of the tax within the city; the city in turn gained the enormous benefit of having its costly street maintenance function taken over by the parish.

21 Some of the ways in which the new government did affect some of the agencies responsible for these programs are discussed in later sections of this monograph.

22 *State* ex rel. *Kemp* v. *City of Baton Rouge*, 215 La. 315, 40 So. (2d) 477 (1949). For a full summary of the case see Rhodes, "The Baton Rouge City-Parish Consolidation," 149-57. The early date at which the suit was filed was advantageous to the plan of government be-

cause it effectively forestalled the threat of litigation by the opponents of the new government, a situation which might have led to chaotic delays.

23 *Bardwell et al.* v. *Parish Council of East Baton Rouge*, 216 La. 537, 44 So. (2d) 107 (1949).

24 *Webb* v. *Parish Council of East Baton Rouge, et al.*, 217 La. 537, 44 So. (2d) 107 (1949).

25 Mayor-President Webb was never completely satisfied with the plan in its existing form. However, toward the close of his administration, shortly before his fatal accident in the spring of 1956, he commented: "We have one of the finest municipal governments in the country and I would be among the first to oppose changes in the basic plan." Although indicating that he favored the commission form and thought the Mayor-President should have more authority, he was opposed to getting into "... a fight which would destroy the plan." Quoted in Rhodes, "The Baton Rouge City-Parish Consolidation," 242.

26 Report of the Plan of Government Study Committee 1956, p: 2.

27 Report of the Plan of Government Study Committee to the City-Parish Councils, June, 1960, p. 10.

Chapter III

1 *Plan of Government of the Parish of East Baton Rouge and the City of Baton Rouge* (Baton Rouge: City Parish Government, 1957), secs. 10.01 *et seq.*

2 State laws did not allow parish zoning at the time of adoption of the plan. *The Plan of Government*, however, authorized the parish planning commission to serve as the zoning commission in the event of state action granting the power, which has subsequently occurred. See the following discussion of zoning.

3 Plan of Government, sec. 10.01(a).

4 *Ibid.*

5 *Minute Book of the Planning Commission* (Baton Rouge: Planning Commission, 1953), II. Minutes of February 20, 1950 list the six committees.

6 See *1949-1959: Ten Years of Progress* (Baton Rouge: City-Parish Planning Commission, 1959), 8, and a memorandum from the planning director to the office of public relations dated December 7, 1959.

7 Bartholomew and Associates, *The Master City-Parish Plan*, 9.

8 City-Parish Planning Commission, *1949-1962, Changing Patterns* (Baton Rouge, 1962). This is an over-sized brochure with unnumbered pages; hereinafter cited *Changing Patterns.*

9 City-Parish Planning Commission, *Population* (Baton Rouge, 1959), 1.

10 Compiled by city-parish planning commission, July, 1962.

11 Table "City Growth, 1840-1960," *Changing Patterns.*

12 Compiled by city-parish planning commission, July, 1962.

13 Percentage taken from *Population*, 1, and *Changing Patterns.*

14 *Changing Patterns.*
15 *Plan of Government*, sec. 10.01 (b).
16 See *Land Use and Zoning Study; Completion Report* (Baton Rouge: City-Parish Planning Commission, 1958), 2-3; *1949-1959: Ten Years of Progress*, 11-12.
17 *Land Use and Zoning Study; Completion Report*, exhibit F.
18 *Ibid.*, exhibit I.
19 City-Parish Zoning Ordinance, sec. 2.212.
20 City-Parish Subdivision Ordinance, sec. V. 1. (b), 3.
21 *Changing Patterns.*
22 Memorandum to members of planning commission from director on action on requests and utilization of map changes dated February 8, 1961, p. 2. See also *1961 Planning Commission Activities and an Outline for 1962* (mimeographed n.d.), 5.
23 *Changing Patterns.*
24 *Land Use and Zoning Study; Completion Report*, 16.
25 This slowdown is attributable to "FHA limitations on financing the backlog of available lots, and general economic conditions." *1961 Planning Commission Activities and an Outline for 1962*, 5.
26 Minutes of the planning commission, February 2, 1950.
27 Observation by first planning engineer in an interview.
28 City-Parish Subdivision Ordinance, sec. VIII (1).
29 *Ibid.*, sec. VIII (1).
30 *Minute Book of the Planning Commission*, 67.
31 *Ibid.*, p. 69. This cites the minutes of the citizens advisory committee meeting on March 30, 1950.
32 *Ibid.*, 88, 92.
33 A review of the minutes for the period April 17 to June 19, 1950 is the basis of this observation; the opinion is also held by the present planning engineer.
34 *Minute Book of the Planning Commission*, 67.
35 *Ibid.*, 67.
36 The hearing was conducted in the East Baton Rouge Parish Courthouse on May 9, 1950, at which time citizens were able to voice their criticisms of the plan.
37 *Minute Book of the Planning Commission*, 71.
38 The only discussion of the parish road plan concerned adding Essen Lane to the specified roads to be included, and that which did occur seemed to be prompted by the hopeful consideration that if Essen Lane were "added we may be able to get it paved by the state." *Minute Book of the Planning Commission*, 75.
39 Planning Director Richard A. McEwen believes this to be the most obvious result of adoption of this type of major road plan.
40 *Minute Book of the Planning Commission*, 75.
41 *Changing Patterns.*
42 Bartholomew and Associates, *The Master City-Parish Plan*, 1.
43 The state constitution prohibited zoning outside the city limits. This restriction was removed, however, in 1956, by constitutional amend-

ment, and because the plan of government had foreseen this development, the duty was assumed by the planning commission.

44 On the value of the first parish road plan as suggested above, the planning engineer of that time, William Singleton, remarked that although the adoption of the plan was not intended to be an educational experience, it later proved to serve that purpose.

45 *Master Plan, Parish Streets and Roads, 1956* (Baton Rouge: City-Parish Planning Commission, 1956), 4; hereinafter cited as *Master Plan.*

46 *Minute Book of the Planning Commission,* minutes for October 1,

47 *Changing Patterns.*

48 *Master Plan,* 6.

49 *Ibid.,* 4.

50 See map, Figure XI, courtesy of the planning commission.

51 *Master Plan,* 4-6.

52 *Ibid.,* 5

53 *Ibid.,* 7

54 For an overall survey of parish road construction, improvements, and extensions, see the following chapter.

55 *Master Plan,* 10.

56 These figures were prepared by the commission staff at the writers' request. Their preparation represents the first statistical evaluation of the road plan's progress by the commission.

57 *Plan of Government,* sec. 11.10-12.02.

58 While this statement is largely conjectural, it is based on the substantial opinion of a sufficient number of persons in or close to local government to be probable and not merely plausible.

59 *Plan of Government,* sec. 11.04-11.09.

60 City-Parish Subdivision Ordinance, 6.

61 *Minute Book of the Planning Commission.*

62 *Master Plan 1956, School, Parks and Playground* (Baton Rouge: City-Parish Planning Commission, 1956), introduction.

63. *Ibid.,* 4.

64 Conclusion of Planning Director McEwen in an interview on July 5, 1962.

65 See Regulations Governing the Subdivision of Land in City of Baton Rouge, April 27, 1949, Paragraph 4 (j).

66 Memorandum to members of the planning commission from the planning director.

67 A previous policy agreement of December 16, 1955, was an elaboration of the relationship between sec. VII of the City-Parish Subdivision Ordinance and the *Master Plan 1956, School, Parks and Playgrounds.* Mimeographed letter dated December 16, 1955, from the office of the planning commission to Dr. Lloyd Funchess, superintendent of the school board, and Ralph Hileman, superintendent of the recreation and parks commission.

68 Table prepared from maps and data on file in the office of the planning commission, supplemented by information gained through dis-

cussions with staff members of the commission and the school board.

69 Interview with Jules Roux, July 16, 1962.

70 *Plan of Government,* sec. 10.04. The other enumerated power relates to zoning.

71 *State Times,* July 29, 1953, p. 1.

72 Interview with Planning Director McEwen, August 2, 1962.

73 Citizens for Greater Baton Rouge, *Your Citizens Plan for a Greater Baton Rouge* (Baton Rouge: Ortlieb Press, 1957).

CHAPTER IV

1 A budget of $425,00 was approved in December, 1946 for the department's operations in 1947, but the jury allocated $50,000 more on September 8, 1947.

2 Interviews with A. H. Harelson, present superintendent of rural bridge and canal maintenance at Baker on July 20, 1962.

3 *Morning Advocate,* September 9, 1947, p. 1

4 *Ibid.,* July 22, 1947, p. 7.

5 *State Times,* March 14, 1945.

6 *Morning Advocate,* August 2, 1947, p. 1.

7 Interview with T. N. Samuel, July 20, 1962, at Baker.

8 Citizens for Greater Baton Rouge, *Program for Progress for Baton Rouge* (Baton Rouge: Franklin Press, 1957).

9 *Morning Advocate,* December 18, 1947, p. 1.

10 *Ibid.,* March 14, 1947, p. 1.

11 *Ibid.,* December 3, 1947, p. 1.

12 *State Times,* January 1, 1949.

13 *Ibid.*

14 *Plan of Government,* sec. 5.01.

15 *Ibid.,* sec. 5.04.

16 Interview with A. M. Rosenthal, Jr., director of the department of public works, on June 26, 1962.

17 *Plan of Government,* sec. 5.02.

18 Interview with A. H. Harelson, superintendent of the rural bridge, canal, and sewer maintenance division on July 20, 1962.

19 "City-Parish Annual Report, 1951," *Morning Advocate,* January 11, 1952.

20 According to the 1958 annual report of the department of public works, rural streets and roads maintenance kept up 360 miles of gravel and over 40 miles of blacktop. Since 1958, 20 miles of gravel roads have been blacktopped.

21 For a more detailed breakdown, see the 1959 annual report of the department of public works.

22 Interview with T. N. Samuel, superintendent of rural streets and roads, July 20, 1962.

23 Inventory of the department of public works for July, 1962, made by the accounting division.

24 Interview with Morgan Fairchild, foreman of the asphalt unit, August 16, 1962.
25 Interview with T. N. Samuel, July 20, 1962.
26 "City-Parish Annual Report, 1958," *Morning Advocate*, March 10, 1959.
27 Interview with A. H. Harelson, July 20, 1962.
28 "City-Parish Annual Report, 1960," *Morning Advocate* (Baton Rouge), February 28, 1961.
29 Interview with A. H. Harelson, July 20, 1962.
30 *Plan of Government*, sec. 1.04.
31 *1949-1959: Ten Years of Progress*, 13.

CHAPTER V

1 Per capita costs were computed by dividing city expenditures by the corresponding city population, parish expenditures by the corresponding rural population, and total parish expenditures by total population.
2 Frederick B. Stocker, *Revenues and Expenditures of State and Local Governments in the Great Plains*, "Agricultural Economics Report," No. 22 (USDA, ERS, FED: Washington, D. C., 1963), 4.
3 Memorandum by Parish Attorney R. Gordon Kean, Jr., *Memorandum Relative to the Plan of Government for the Parish of East Baton Rouge and City of Baton Rouge* (mimeographed, n.d.), 8-9.
4 Recipient agencies are indicated in Appendix Tables 23 and 24.
5 Bureau of the Census, Department of Commerce, *U. S. Census of Agriculture for Louisiana, 1959* (Washington, 1960), 151.
6 Computed by applying parish-wide millage rates shown in Table 13, plus state tax of 5.75 mills. Excludes special district taxes but includes rates for schools, recreation, and courthouse. See Figure XXIV.
7 Louisiana Homestead Exemption Law.
8 *Acts of the Legislature*, Act 401 (1946).
9 An Iowa study reported cost of county government, including schools, in 1959 at $50.25 per capita. Metropolitan and urban-center counties had lower per capita costs – about $35 – and in rural counties with declining populations the cost was about $91 per capita. Robert I. Wessel, "Iowa County Governments Face Different Problems," *Iowa Farm Science*, Vol. XVII, No. 8 (February, 1963), 17.

CHAPTER VI

1 Quoted in Rhodes, "The Baton Rouge City-Parish Consolidation," 185.
2 See a report on these views in James H. Hughes, Jr., "Consolidated Government Suits Both Rural and Urban Interest," *County Officer*, Vol. 24, No. 8 (April, 1963), 148-49.

3 After considering a proposed plan to permit annexation through the initiative of the city council, the 1951 study committee concluded that annexation could take place by amending the *Plan of Government* to redefine the city boundaries as set forth in sec. 1.08 (a).

4 For a fuller review of some of these services during the first ten years under the *Plan*, see the undated *Memorandum Relative to the Plan of Government for the Parish of East Baton Rouge and City of Baton Rouge, Louisiana* by R. Gordon Kean, especially pp. 8-9 and n. 25, p. 12. Kean reports the addition of nine new fire stations and a new fire alarm headquarters, and the installation of 2,500 fire hydrants in the new area of the city. Baton Rouge is now the only city in Louisiana, and one of only three in the south which is classified second class by the National Board of Fire Underwriters. Changes in police administration, traffic circulation management, building codes, etc., have been based on surveys by professional organizations of the highest standings.

5 Quoted in Hughes, "Consolidated Government Suits Both Rural and Urban Interest," *loc. cit.*

Index